THE JUNIOR
BIBLE

scandinavia

THE JUNIOR BIBLE

1st edition, 3rd print
Copyright © 2023 by Scandinavia Publishing House
Drejervej 15, DK-2400 Copenhagen NV, Denmark
info@sph.as | www.sph.as
Text by Andrew Newton
Illustrations by Fabiano Fiorin
Designed by Gao Hanyu

ISBN 9788772032122
Printed in China

THIS BOOK BELONGS TO

....

GIVEN TO ME BY

....

ON

....

THE JUNIOR
BIBLE

RETOLD BY ANDREW NEWTON
ILLUSTRATED BY FABIANO FIORIN

scandinavia

CONTENTS

THE NEW TESTAMENT

THE
OLD TESTAMENT

IN THE BEGINNING

GENESIS 1:1-2:7, 18-25

Way back before anything else
existed, God was. He always existed and
always will exist. In the very beginning,
God decided to make something—a world,
a universe, a beautiful place where people
could live with Him and love Him and be loved
by Him. He created the heavens and the earth.
This new creation was covered in darkness, so God
spoke into the darkness and said, "Let there be
light." Dazzling light burst forth and pushed the
darkness back. God separated the light from
the darkness, making the first day and the
first night.

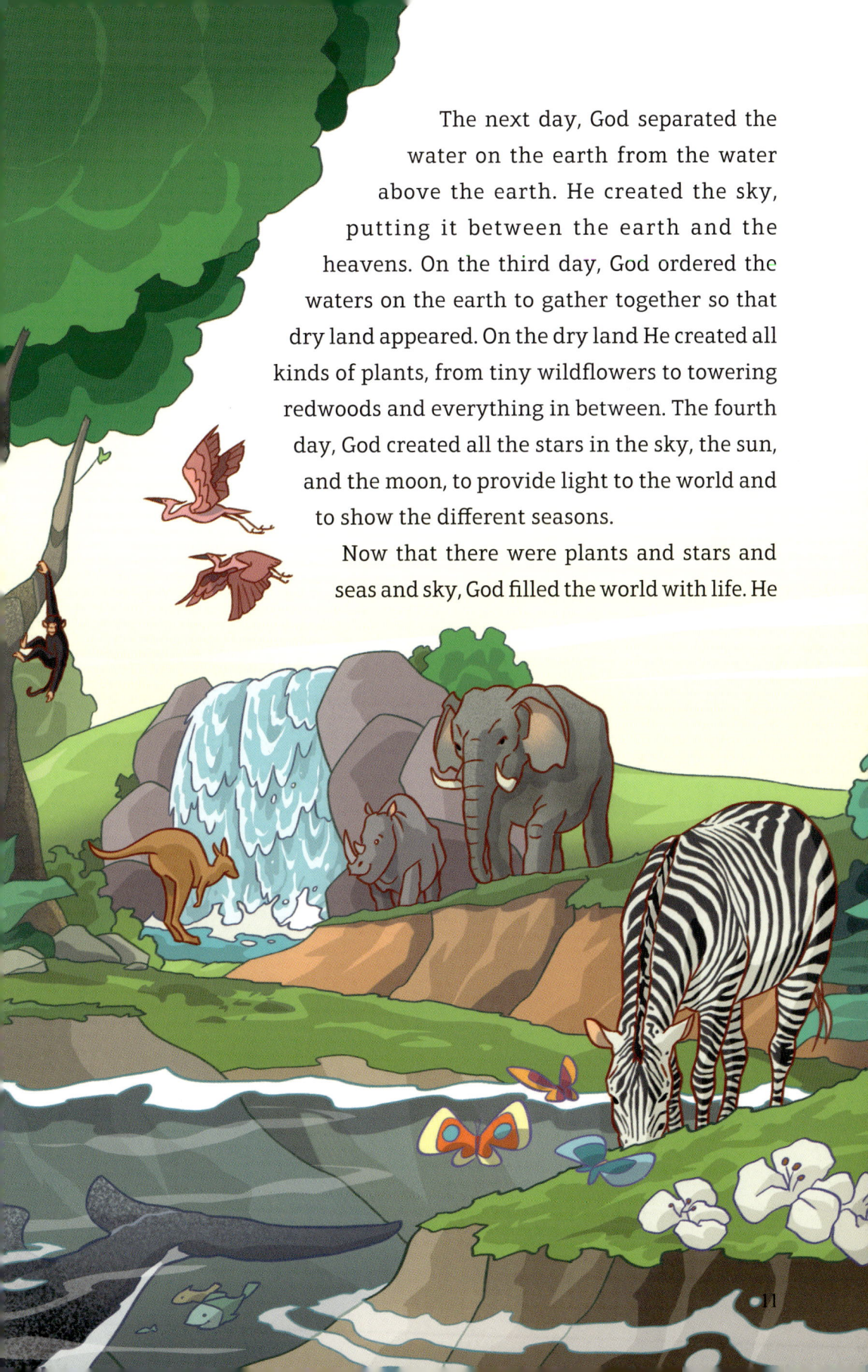

The next day, God separated the water on the earth from the water above the earth. He created the sky, putting it between the earth and the heavens. On the third day, God ordered the waters on the earth to gather together so that dry land appeared. On the dry land He created all kinds of plants, from tiny wildflowers to towering redwoods and everything in between. The fourth day, God created all the stars in the sky, the sun, and the moon, to provide light to the world and to show the different seasons.

Now that there were plants and stars and seas and sky, God filled the world with life. He created all the birds of the sky and all the creatures of the sea, blessing them and telling them to multiply and fill the seas and the sky. On the sixth day, God made all the animals that live on the ground, from the smallest ant to the tallest giraffe. He blessed the animals, too, and told them to multiply and fill the world. Last of all, God wanted to make someone who could live with Him and love Him and be loved by Him, someone who could take care of the world He had made. So God made a man in His own image, with a mind, a heart, and a soul. He formed the man out of the dust of the ground and breathed His own breath into the man's lungs, and Adam, the first man, breathed his first breath.

God saw that it wasn't good for Adam to be alone, so He made Adam fall into a deep sleep. While Adam was sleeping, God took out one of his ribs and used it to make the first woman, then sealed up Adam's side again. When Adam woke up, he was overjoyed to see the woman God had made. She was beautiful, and she was like him—a perfect partner. He said, "At last, here is bone of my bone and flesh of my flesh!"

Adam and his wife, Eve, lived with God in a gorgeous garden He had planted for them. They were naked, but they didn't feel ashamed about it. Everything in their new home was perfect; there was no sin and no shame. God looked around at everything He had made, and He saw that it was all very good. On the seventh day, God rested from His work of creation. His new world was complete, and it was full of creatures and people to live with Him and love Him and be loved by Him.

OUT OF EDEN
GENESIS 2:15-16; 3:1-23

God gave Adam and Eve one rule to follow: "You may eat fruit from any tree in this garden, except for the tree in the middle of the garden. If you eat from that tree, you will die."

The serpent wanted to trick Adam and Eve into disobeying God. He slithered over to Eve and said, "Did God really say you cannot eat from any of these trees?"

"No," Eve answered. "We can eat from any tree except the one in the middle of the garden. If we eat its fruit, we will die."

"You will not die," he hissed. "God knows if you eat that fruit, you will be wise like Him. He's lying to you!"

Eve saw that the fruit looked delicious. She picked a piece and took a bite, then gave some to Adam, too. He took a big bite, then they realized they were naked. Adam and Eve hurried to make coverings for themselves out of leaves. While they were working, they heard God approaching. They were ashamed of disobeying Him, so they hid in some bushes.

"Adam," God called, "where are you?"

"I heard you coming," Adam said, "and I hid because I was naked."

"Who told you you were naked?" God asked. "Did you eat from the tree I commanded you not to eat from?"

"It was Eve! She gave me some of the fruit," Adam said.

"What have you done?" God asked Eve.

"The serpent tricked me!" Eve exclaimed.

God turned to the serpent and said, "You will be cursed for this. I will make you and Eve bitter enemies. Her descendant will crush your head, and you will bruise His heel."

Because Adam and Eve had sinned, they could no longer live in the perfect garden with God. Instead, they would live outside the garden and work hard to grow food out of the dry ground, and they would experience pain and death. But

God still wanted people to live with Him and love Him and be loved by Him. He killed an animal to make clothes for Adam and Eve, and He had a plan to cover the sins of His people and make it so they could live with Him again.

THE FIRST MURDER

GENESIS 4:1-16

Life was hard outside the garden, but it was about to get harder. Before long, Adam and Eve had two sons named Cain and Abel. Cain was a farmer, and Abel was a shepherd. One day, the brothers were bringing offerings to God. Cain brought some produce from his garden, and Abel brought a lamb from his flock. God was pleased with Abel and his offering, but not with Cain.

When Cain saw that God was only pleased with Abel's offering, he was furious. He told Abel, "Let's go into this field."

God knew Cain's heart, and He said, "Why are you upset? If you do what is right, I will accept you, too. Be careful: sin wants to master you. Don't let it."

Cain ignored God's warning. He attacked Abel and killed him, burying his body in the field. God punished Cain by making him wander the earth, never able to settle down. Cain was afraid that his punishment was too harsh, that anyone who found him would kill him, but God promised He would punish anyone who harmed Cain.

Unfortunately, this was not to be the last murder. Sin was now part of the world, and people's hearts were twisted with evil desires. God still wanted to live with people who would love Him and be loved by Him, but very few people wanted to love and obey God. Most just wanted to sin, choosing their own will and desires over God's.

STARTING OVER
GENESIS 6:5-9:17

Only a few generations after Adam and Eve, the world was full of people who didn't care about God or anyone else. They only wanted to do evil, selfish things all the time. God saw this evil, and He was sad He had made people in the first place. He decided to start over by destroying all the living things He had made. Noah was the only person who loved God and tried to live with Him and obey Him. God appeared to Noah and said, "The people of the world have become so evil that I am going to destroy them with a flood. Build a huge boat, an ark. Make it three stories tall, and put a door in the side. I will destroy everything that breathes, but I promise to keep you and your family safe in the ark. You must gather two of every kind of animal that walks on the ground or flies in the air, a male and a female, and seven of every clean animal that I accept as a sacrifice. Put them in the ark with you so that they will be safe from the flood."

Noah obeyed everything God told him. He had three sons: Shem, Ham, and Japheth, and they were all married. Noah and his sons worked for a long time, and they finally finished the ark. God told Noah, "Get ready

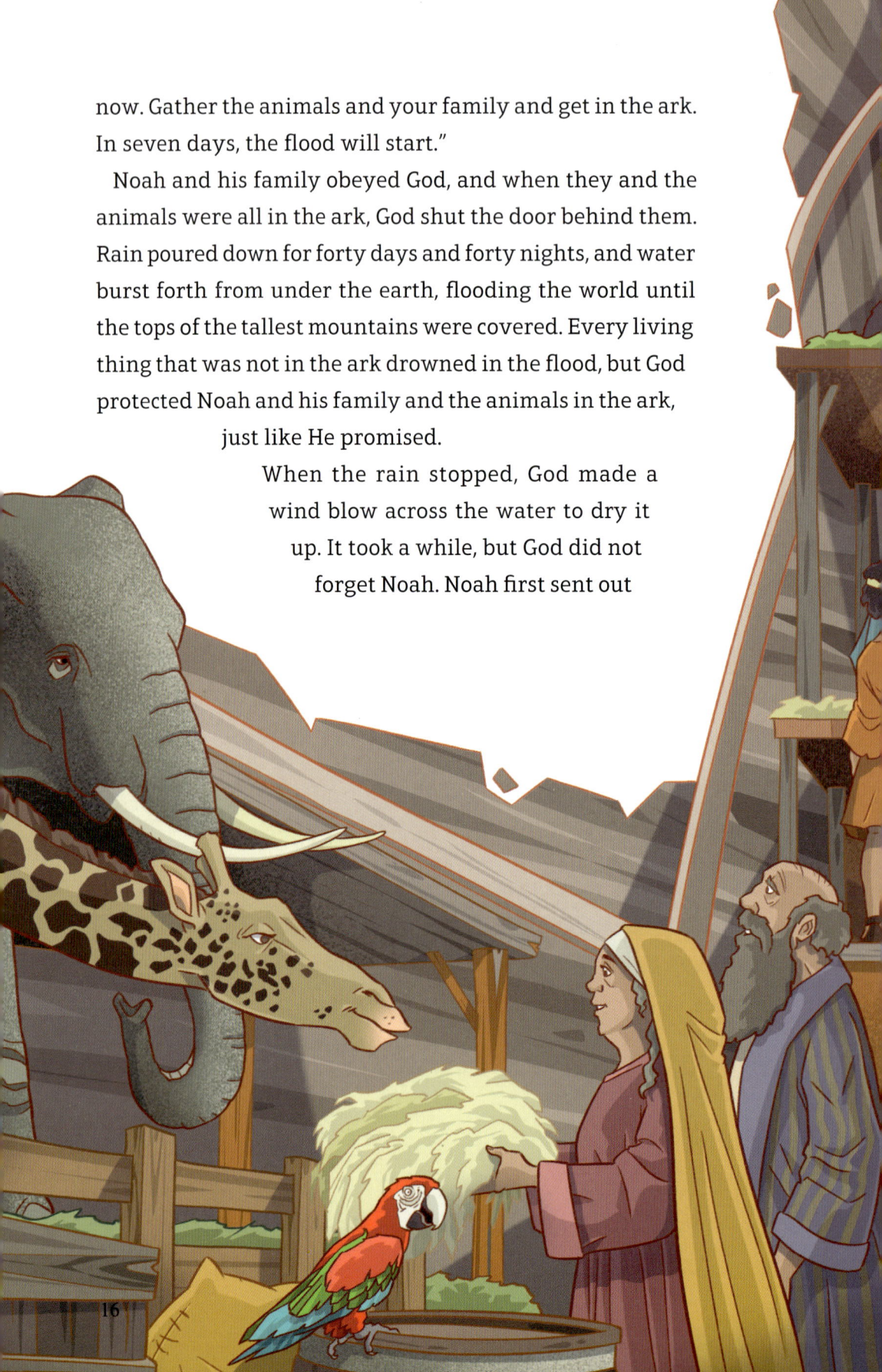

now. Gather the animals and your family and get in the ark. In seven days, the flood will start."

Noah and his family obeyed God, and when they and the animals were all in the ark, God shut the door behind them. Rain poured down for forty days and forty nights, and water burst forth from under the earth, flooding the world until the tops of the tallest mountains were covered. Every living thing that was not in the ark drowned in the flood, but God protected Noah and his family and the animals in the ark, just like He promised.

When the rain stopped, God made a wind blow across the water to dry it up. It took a while, but God did not forget Noah. Noah first sent out

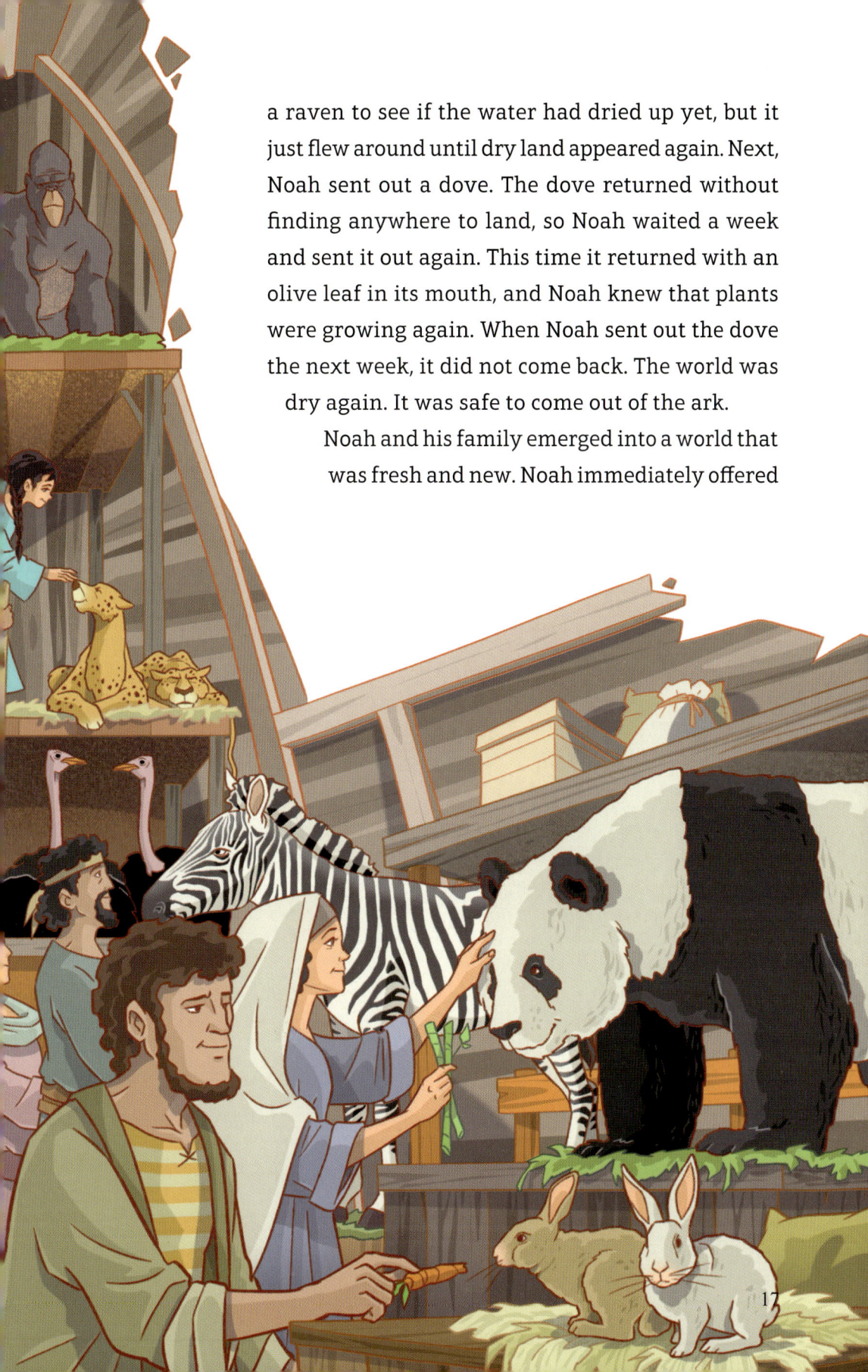

a raven to see if the water had dried up yet, but it just flew around until dry land appeared again. Next, Noah sent out a dove. The dove returned without finding anywhere to land, so Noah waited a week and sent it out again. This time it returned with an olive leaf in its mouth, and Noah knew that plants were growing again. When Noah sent out the dove the next week, it did not come back. The world was dry again. It was safe to come out of the ark.

Noah and his family emerged into a world that was fresh and new. Noah immediately offered

17

sacrifices to God, using some of the clean animals. He burned them on an altar to thank God for saving them from the flood. God was pleased with Noah and the sacrifice. There was a rainbow in the sky, and God said, "The rainbow will be a sign of my promise that I am making to you and every living thing, Noah. I promise that I will never flood the earth and destroy every living thing again. Whenever you see a rainbow in the sky, you can remember my promise. Now, I want you and your family to multiply. Grow and spread out to fill the world with people again." God was starting over with Noah's family, and He wanted to have a relationship with them. They loved God and wanted to live with Him, but sin is present in every human heart, even in those who love God.

A TOWER TO HEAVEN

GENESIS 11:1-9

Noah's descendants began to multiply, but they didn't spread out. Even though God commanded the people to spread over all the earth, they wanted to stay in one place and build themselves a city that would protect them and make them famous. They began building a tower that would reach up to heaven using bricks and tar.

When God saw the tower, He said, "If these people succeed at building this tower, they will be so confident that they won't seek after me. They'll think nothing is impossible for them. I will put a stop to their arrogance."

So God went down and confused the people by making them speak different languages. The workers could not understand each other anymore, so the people had to give up on their city. They scattered across the world like God had ordered them to do in the first place.

GOD MAKES A PROMISE
GENESIS 12:1-9; 15:1-7; 17:4-5

God appeared to a man named Abram, a distant descendant of Noah, and said, "Leave your homeland and go to the place that I will show you. I will bless you and make your descendants into a great nation. Everyone who blesses you, I will bless, and I will curse anyone who curses you. Everyone on earth will be blessed through you."

Abram believed God and set out for the place God told him to go. Abram and his wife Sarai, along with their nephew Lot, went all the way to the land of Canaan, where God said, "I will give this land to you and to your descendants after you forever."

Many years later, God appeared to Abram again and said, "I will give you a great reward, Abram!"

Now Abram didn't have any children, so he said, "Lord, what good will this reward be, since I will leave all of my possessions to one of my servants?"

God answered, "No, you won't! You will have a son, you and your wife Sarai. You will have so many descendants that they will be more numerous than the stars in the sky. I am changing your name and your wife's name. Your name will now be Abraham, because you are the father of many nations, and Sarai's name will be Sarah." Abraham believed God, and God was pleased with him. This promise was the beginning of a new way for God to have a relationship with people. Through covenants, God could make Himself known and give people a way to love Him and be loved by Him and live with Him.

21

GOD RESCUES LOT

GENESIS 18:1-19:29

Abraham's nephew Lot had gone to live in a city called Sodom, and Abraham was camped several miles to the north. God visited Abraham and repeated His promise that Abraham and Sarah would have a son. As He was leaving, God told Abraham, "There has been such a loud outcry against the people of Sodom that I am sending my angels to investigate the city. If it is as evil as I've heard, then I am going to destroy the whole place."

Abraham's heart grew heavy because he was worried about Lot, but he was afraid to talk back to God. He said, "Lord, please don't be angry with me, but will you destroy the innocent along with the wicked? If you find fifty righteous people in the city, will you spare the whole place for their sake?"

God answered, "If I find fifty righteous people, I will spare the city."

"Lord, don't be angry, since I've already spoken to you. What if you only find forty-five righteous people? Will you destroy the whole place for the lack of five?"

"If I find forty-five, I will spare the city," God promised.

Abraham asked again if God would spare the city for forty, thirty, twenty, and finally ten. Each time, God promised that He would spare the city if He found that many righteous people there.

The angels arrived in Sodom in the evening, and Lot saw them in the town square. He invited them into his home, insisting that they not spend the night out in the square. That night, all the men in the city came to Lot's house and demanded to see the two angels so they could do horrible things to them. Lot refused, and the angels made the men of the city blind so they couldn't hurt Lot.

In the morning, the angels took Lot and his wife and their two daughters out of the city. They told them, "Run to the hills and do not stop or look back, because God is going to destroy the city for all the evil its people have committed."

Lot and his daughters fled to the hills, but his wife looked back and she turned into a pillar of salt. God sent down fire and burning sulfur from heaven and totally destroyed Sodom and the wicked people who lived there. God had not even found ten people in Sodom who loved Him and wanted to have a relationship with Him.

GOD WILL PROVIDE
GENESIS 21:1-7; 22:1-18

God kept his promise to Abraham and Sarah, and Sarah gave birth to a baby boy, even though she and Abraham were very old. They named their son Isaac, and said, "Everyone will laugh with us when they hear how God has blessed us!"

When Isaac was a young man God said, "Abraham, take your son, Isaac, whom you love, and offer him as a burnt offering on a mountain I will show you."

The next morning, Abraham got up early, chopped wood, and took Isaac with him to go find the mountain God had told him about. A servant went with them, leading a donkey. When they reached the mountain, Abraham said, "The boy and I will go on from here. We will offer a sacrifice to God, and then we will return to you."

Abraham was carrying a knife and a torch, and Isaac was carrying the wood. When they were part of the way up the mountain, Isaac asked, "Father, we have fire and wood, but where is the lamb for the burnt offering?"

Abraham said, "God Himself will provide the lamb, my son."

They reached the top of the mountain, and Abraham built an altar out of the stones he found there. When he was finished, he tied up Isaac and placed him on the altar. Abraham trusted God, but he was terrified as he raised the knife, ready to kill the son he had waited so long for.

"Stop!" God's angel called out. "Don't hurt the boy! God knows that you trust Him enough that you would not keep back even your only son from Him."

Abraham untied Isaac, then he saw a ram stuck in the nearby bushes by its horns. He took the ram and offered it on the altar instead of Isaac. God's angel repeated God's promises to Abraham, and Abraham named that place "God will provide." He went back home with his son, even more certain that God would fulfill His promises and take care of him and Isaac. When God makes a promise, He keeps it, no matter what. God provided for Abraham and Isaac, and He continues to provide for people who love Him and want to have a relationship with Him. Much later, on the same mountain, God would provide a sacrifice that would make it possible for people to finally be forgiven of their sins and live with God, loving Him and being loved by Him.

THE MATCHMAKER

GENESIS 24

By the time Isaac was ready to get married, Abraham was very old. He called his head servant to him and said, "I want you to make me a promise. Swear it by the Lord, the God of heaven and earth. Promise you will find a wife for my son Isaac from my own people. Do not let him marry a woman from here in Canaan."

"What if no woman from your homeland will come here to marry Isaac?" the servant asked. "Should I bring him back there to live?"

"No! Do not bring my son back there," Abraham said. "This is the land that God has promised to give to my family, so Isaac must not return to the land of my fathers. If there is no one who will come to Canaan to marry Isaac, you will be free from your oath."

"I swear by the Lord your God that I will do what you have said," the servant promised.

He set out right away, taking along camels loaded with gifts for Abraham's relatives. When he arrived at the city where Abraham's family lived, the servant stopped by the well outside the city. He looked up to heaven and prayed, "Lord God, please show your love and faithfulness to my master Abraham by giving me success today. When a young woman comes out to draw water, I will say to her, 'Please give me some water to drink.' Let the woman you have chosen to come marry Isaac reply, 'Drink, and I will water your camels also.' Then I will know that you have shown your love to my master."

Before he had even finished praying, Rebekah, a descendant of Abraham's brother, came out with her jar to draw water from the well. She was beautiful, single, and the right age for marriage. The servant went over to her and said, "Please, young lady, will you give me some water to drink?"

Rebekah gave the servant water from her jar and said, "Drink, sir, and I will water your camels until they have had enough also."

When Rebekah had finished watering the camels, the servant asked her about her family. When she said that she was related to Abraham's brother, he praised God for showing faithful love to Abraham by leading him to the right person.

Rebekah took the servant home to meet her family, and he told them about his mission, how he was looking for a young woman who would come marry Isaac and live in Canaan, the land God had promised to give to Abraham's descendants. Then he gave them all the gifts he had brought. Rebekah's family talked it over, then gave her their blessing to do whatever she felt was best.

"Do you want to go with this man to marry Isaac?" they asked her.

"I do," Rebekah answered.

Rebekah traveled back to Canaan, where she met Isaac for the first time. They got married soon after that. God had shown His faithful love to Abraham and his family. He had provided and would continue to provide, just as He promised.

HEEL-GRABBER
GENESIS 25:19-26; 25:27-34; 27:1-40

Before long, Isaac and Rebekah had twin boys. They named the firstborn Esau. The second boy was born with his hand grabbing Esau's heel, so they named him Jacob, which means "heel-grabber." The boys grew into young men, and they couldn't be more different. Esau loved to hunt; he was a rugged, hairy outdoorsman. Jacob, on the other hand, liked to farm and raise his father's sheep and goats, staying close to home. Isaac loved Esau the most, but Rebekah had a special place in her heart for Jacob.

One day, Jacob was making stew when Esau got home from hunting. He was very hungry.

"Jacob," Esau said, "give me some of that stew! I'm about to pass out from hunger!"

Now, Jacob was smart and sneaky, so he saw an opportunity to trick his brother. As the firstborn, even if only by a few minutes, Esau's inheritance would be twice as big as Jacob's. Jacob decided to see just how desperate Esau was for some food. He said, "I will sell you a bowl of stew. All it will cost is your birthright as the oldest son."

"What good is my birthright if I starve to death?" Esau exclaimed.

"Swear an oath that you are transferring your rights as the firstborn to me," Jacob insisted.

"Fine," Esau said, "just give me some of that stew!"

Jacob had gotten the better end of that deal by far, but he wasn't done with his sneaky ways yet.

When Isaac had gotten so old that he couldn't see, he told Esau, "I am going to die soon. Now, go out and hunt some wild game and prepare my favorite meal for me. Then come serve it to me so I can bless you."

Rebekah overheard Isaac talking to Esau, so she went and found Jacob. "Listen to me," she told him, "and you will receive a great blessing. Go and kill two young goats from the herd and bring them to me. I will prepare your father's favorite meal and you will serve it to him, pretending to be Esau. Then he will bless you instead of your brother."

"But what if he smells me when I am serving him the food?" Jacob asked. "He will be able to tell the difference. Besides, Esau is hairier than I am. What if he touches my arms?"

"Put on some of Esau's clothes so that you will smell like him," Rebekah answered. "I will give you the skins of the goats to wear on your arms. That way, if he touches you, he will think you are hairy."

Jacob and Rebekah put their plan into motion. Before Esau got back from hunting, Jacob entered Isaac's tent with a bowl of his father's favorite food, disguised as Esau.

"Is that you, Esau?" Isaac asked. "How can you be back so soon?"

"It is, father," Jacob lied. "The Lord your God blessed me and I was successful in the hunt. Now eat this food so you can bless me."

"Come closer," Isaac said. Jacob approached to serve Isaac the food. Isaac took a deep breath and smelled Esau's clothes that Jacob was wearing. He put his hand on Jacob's arm and felt the hairy goatskins. "The voice is Jacob's voice," Isaac said, "but I smell my son Esau. His scent is like the smell of the open field. And these hairy arms could not belong to anyone but him." So Isaac blessed Jacob in the name of the Lord, promising that he would inherit the promises that God had given Abraham.

When Esau returned from hunting and brought Isaac food, Isaac was confused. He said, "If you are Esau, then who just left after receiving my blessing? Because that person will be blessed."

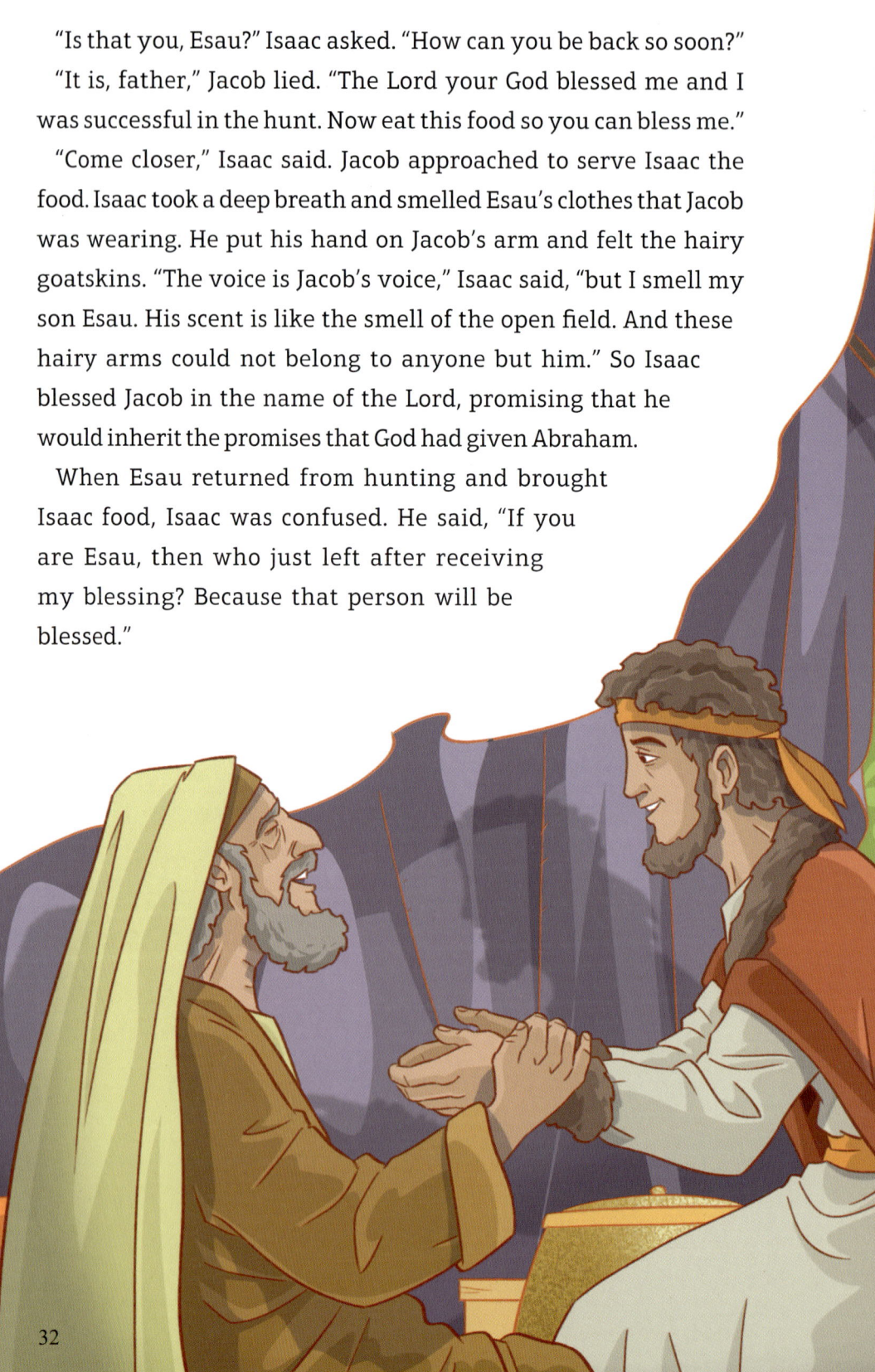

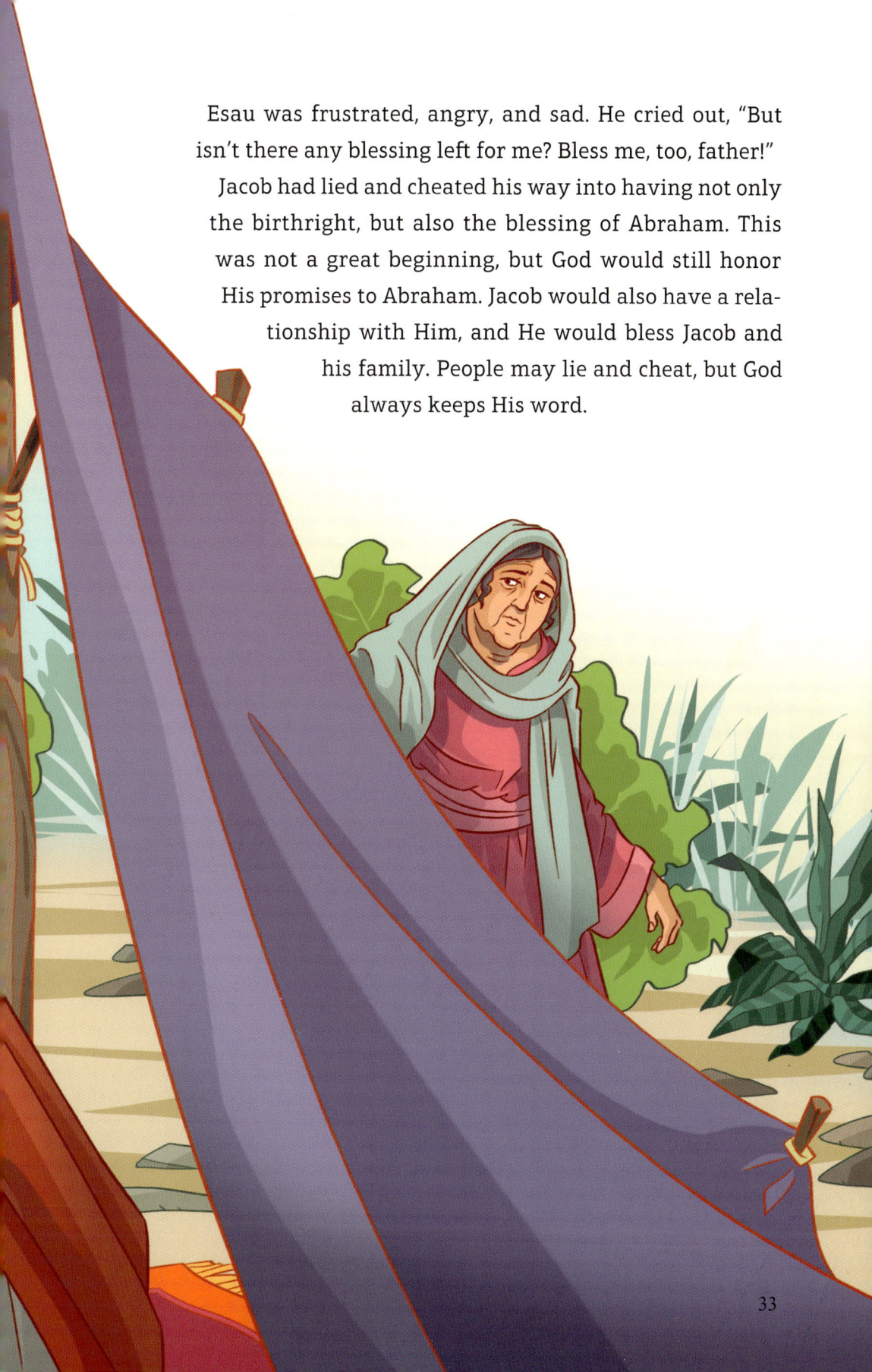

Esau was frustrated, angry, and sad. He cried out, "But isn't there any blessing left for me? Bless me, too, father!"

Jacob had lied and cheated his way into having not only the birthright, but also the blessing of Abraham. This was not a great beginning, but God would still honor His promises to Abraham. Jacob would also have a relationship with Him, and He would bless Jacob and his family. People may lie and cheat, but God always keeps His word.

AN ANGELIC WRESTLING MATCH

GENESIS 27:41-45; 32:3-31

Esau was so angry with Jacob that he wanted to kill him. Rebekah found out about it, and sent Jacob to live with her brother in her homeland for a while. While he was there, Jacob married not one, but two women: his cousin Rachel and her sister Leah.

Finally, God told Jacob to return home. He gathered his wives and children, along with his flocks and herds, and set out for Canaan. He was afraid that Esau would still be angry, so he sent servants ahead of him with gifts for his brother. The servants returned and said, "Esau is coming, and there are lots of people with him."

When he heard this, Jacob got even more nervous and afraid. He knelt down and prayed, "Lord, you are the God of my father and grandfather. You told me to return home to my family and you would bless me. You promised to give us this land and make us prosper. I don't deserve the blessings you have given me. When I left here, I was alone, and now I have a family and many animals. You promised that you would make our family as numerous as the stars in the sky, so please keep your promise."

After Jacob prayed, an angel appeared and wrestled with him. They wrestled all night, and the angel said, "Let me go; it is almost dawn."

"I won't let you go unless you bless me," Jacob answered.

"What is your name?" the angel asked.

"Jacob," he replied.

"From now on, you will be called Israel," the angel said, "because you have wrestled with God and men and have been victorious."

When the sun came up, the angel was gone, and Jacob, now named Israel, had a limp from where the angel had struck his hip. The promise God had made to Abraham was coming true. Jacob's family would be the start of a whole nation, a nation that had a relationship with Him.

THE DREAMER

GENESIS 37; 39:1-45:28

Jacob had twelve sons and a daughter. He loved his wife Rachel more than Leah, but Rachel only had two children. Her first was Joseph, and he was Jacob's favorite son. Her second was Benjamin, and she died giving birth to him. Jacob gave Joseph a beautiful robe made from expensive, colorful cloth to show how much he loved him, and Joseph's brothers hated him for it.

To make matters worse, Joseph had strange dreams that he insisted on telling his brothers about. "I had a dream," he said. "We were all out in the field, binding bundles of wheat. Suddenly, my bundle stood straight up, and your bundles all gathered around and bowed down to mine."

"What do you mean?" his brothers asked. "Do you really think we will bow to you?"

Jacob knew that God sometimes talked to people in dreams, so he didn't say anything. He thought about Joseph's dream and wondered what it could mean.

Later, Joseph had another dream. "This time," he said, "I saw the sun, the moon, and eleven stars bowing down to me. Cool, right?"

This time even Jacob was angry with Joseph. "What?" he asked. "Do you think that your mother and I will bow down to you, along with your brothers? This is too much, Joseph." But God had sent Joseph those dreams for a reason.

One day, Joseph's older brothers were watching Jacob's sheep in a field that was a long way from home. Jacob sent Joseph to see what they were doing and report back to him. When the brothers saw Joseph coming, they said, "This is our chance! Let's kills this dreamer and throw his body in one of the empty wells out here. Then we'll see what becomes of his dreams."

But Reuben, the oldest of the brothers, said, "Don't hurt him! Why should we be guilty of murder? Let's throw him into a dry well to teach him a lesson. But don't kill him!" So the brothers took Joseph and ripped off his fancy robe, then they threw him into an empty well in the field.

The brothers were eating lunch when they saw a caravan of traders passing by. They called the men over and said, "Where are you going?"

"South, to Egypt," the traders replied.

"We have an offer for you," the brothers said. "This young man is strong and a good worker. How much will you give us if we sell him to you as a slave?"

"Twenty pieces of silver," the traders answered.

"Deal!" The brothers pulled Joseph back out of the well and sold him to the traders.

Reuben had been away, watching the sheep while the others ate. He had planned

to let Joseph out when he got back, but when he returned to the well, Joseph was gone. Reuben tore his clothes in sorrow and exclaimed, "What did you do? The boy is gone! What am I going to tell father?"

The other brothers had a plan. They ripped Joseph's colorful robe and dipped it in animal blood. When they returned home, they showed it to Jacob and said, "We found this robe. Do you recognize it?"

Jacob wept and wailed. "My son!" he cried. "My son Joseph is dead! He has been killed by wild animals!" Jacob mourned for a long time, refusing to be comforted. "My son is dead," he said. "I will die and be with him."

Meanwhile, in Egypt, the traders sold Joseph to the captain of Pharaoh's guards, a man named Potiphar. Joseph lived in Potiphar's house and took care of it for his master. God was with Joseph, and he was successful at everything he did. Potiphar soon put Joseph in charge of all of his slaves and servants. There was no one in the whole house higher than Joseph except for Potiphar himself.

Potiphar's wife liked Joseph. He was young and handsome, and she wanted to sleep with him. She approached him and said, "Joseph, come to bed with me."

Joseph refused. He said, "How could I do that and betray my master? He trusts me with everything in his house and doesn't keep anything from me except for you, because you are his wife. I could never do such a terrible thing! It would be sinning, not only against my master, but also against God."

Potiphar's wife didn't give up. She kept pestering Joseph, day after day. He kept refusing her advances and wouldn't even come close to her. One day, there was no one else in the house, and Potiphar's wife saw her chance. She grabbed hold of Joseph's coat before he could get away and said, "Come sleep with me!" Joseph didn't even reply. He just ran away, leaving his coat behind in her hand.

When Potiphar got home that night, his wife said, "That Hebrew slave you bought is making fools of us. Today, he tried to force himself on me. When I screamed, he ran and left his coat behind. Here it is!" Potiphar believed his wife's lie and threw Joseph into prison.

Even in prison, God was with Joseph. The head jailor soon put Joseph in charge of other prisoners. While Joseph was there, Pharaoh threw his chief baker and his chief cupbearer into prison because he was angry with them. The head jailor put these new prisoners under Joseph's care.

One night, the baker and the cupbearer both had dreams. They were troubled by their dreams, and they wanted to know what they meant, but no one could interpret the dreams for them. When they told Joseph, he said, "Doesn't God send dreams? And don't interpretations belong to Him? Tell me your dreams."

The cupbearer spoke up first. He said, "I saw a vine with three branches. The branches budded, blossomed, and grew bunches of grapes. I took the grapes and squeezed them into Pharaoh's cup and gave it to him, just like I used to."

"This is what your dream means," Joseph said. "The three branches are three days. Within three days, Pharaoh will forgive you. He will restore you to your old position as chief cupbearer. When he does this, please don't forget about me. I have been in prison for a long time, even though I did nothing wrong. When you are released, please help me get out too."

The baker was excited that the cupbearer's dream had a good interpretation, so he said, "I had a dream too. In my dream, I was carrying three baskets on my head. In the top basket were all kinds of bread and pastries and baked goods. But birds flew down and ate the bread out of the basket."

Joseph felt sorry for the baker, but he told him the truth. He said. "The three baskets are also three days. In three days, Pharaoh will have you

executed. He will hang your body from a pole, and birds will come peck at it. I am sorry, but that is what your dream means."

Three days later, Pharaoh was celebrating his birthday. Just like Joseph had said, he called for the cupbearer and forgave him, restoring him to his former position. He also had the baker executed, just like Joseph had said. Unfortunately, the cupbearer was so happy to be free and have his old position back that he forgot all about Joseph.

It wasn't until two years later that the cupbearer remembered his promise to Joseph. Pharaoh had dreamed two dreams, and no one could tell him what they meant. "I was standing by the Nile river," he said, "when I saw seven fat, healthy cows come up from the river and graze

along the riverbank. Then, seven scrawny, ugly cows came up behind them and swallowed the seven healthy cows whole. The seven scrawny cows didn't look any fatter for having eaten the fat cows. I also dreamed that there were seven plump, ripe heads of grain, and then seven withered, scorched heads of grain appeared and swallowed the seven ripe heads of grain. Can anyone tell me what this means?"

When the cupbearer heard about Pharaoh's dreams, he said, "Your Majesty, I just remembered: When you were angry with me two years ago and threw me in prison with the chief baker, there was a man there with us named Joseph. One night, the baker and I both had strange dreams, and Joseph told us what they meant. Three days later, what Joseph said came true. He can tell you what your dreams mean, I'm sure of it."

"What are we waiting for?" Pharaoh answered. "Bring him here!"

Pharaoh sent new clothes to Joseph, who quickly made himself presentable. When Joseph arrived in the palace, Pharaoh told him, "I dreamed two dreams, and no one can tell me what they mean. My cupbearer tells me that you can interpret dreams."

"I can't do that, Your Majesty," Joseph answered, "but God can. Tell me your dreams, and I will ask God what they mean." Pharaoh told Joseph his dreams, and then Joseph said, "Your Majesty, both of your dreams mean the same thing. God has told you twice so you will know that it will definitely happen. God is telling you about the future. The seven healthy cows and the seven good heads of grain stand for seven years of good harvests, plenty of rain, and abundant food. The seven skinny cows and the seven shriveled heads of grain stand for seven years of famine, drought, and hunger. For seven years, there will be so much food in Egypt that everyone will have far more than they need. After that, there will be seven years of such severe famine that the good years will be forgotten. God has sent you these dreams to warn you about this, so you can prepare.

"Your Majesty, I suggest that you put someone you trust, someone wise, in charge of storing up food during the good years. Collect a fifth of all the harvest during those years and store it up in warehouses to prepare for the coming famine. This way, you will save enough food that Egypt will not starve when the famine comes."

When Joseph finished speaking, Pharaoh conferred with his advisors and said, "Your words are wise, and your advice is sound. I cannot think of anyone better to execute this plan than you. God has put His Spirit on you, and He is with you in everything you do. I hereby make you the second most powerful person in Egypt. You will answer only to me. You will be in charge of collecting food and preparing for the famine."

It all happened like Joseph said. For seven years there was more than enough food, and the harvests were plentiful. Joseph built huge store-houses for the food that he gathered from the people, saving it up so they would have enough to eat during the famine. After the years of plenty, there was a famine so intense that no one in the world was able to grow enough food. Only Egypt had enough food, because Pharaoh had listened to Joseph.

Joseph's brothers heard that there was food in Egypt, so they set out to buy grain for their families. Benjamin stayed behind with Jacob because Jacob was afraid to let him out of his sight. Benjamin was the only son left from Jacob's favorite wife, so he refused to let him go. When the brothers arrived in Egypt, they were brought before Joseph, since Pharaoh had put him in charge of distributing and selling the food he had stored. Joseph recognized his brothers immediately, but they didn't recognize him, since he was dressed like an Egyptian.

The brothers bowed down to Joseph, but he pretended not to know who they were. "You have come to spy on our land and find our weak-nesses!" he said.

"No, sir," the brothers replied. "We are brothers. There were twelve of us, but one is dead and the youngest stayed home with our father."

"You are spies!" Joseph answered. "Unless your other brother comes here, I will not believe you. You will all be prisoners until I see this other brother of yours."

After a few days, Joseph said, "I am a God fearing man, so I will give you a chance to prove yourselves. I will let all but one of you go. I will sell you food for your families, and then you must return here with your other brother to prove you are not spies. When you do, I will release the brother I have kept as a prisoner. Do not return to me again without your younger brother."

Joseph had his brother Simeon tied up and led away, then he ordered his servants to fill the brothers' sacks with grain and put the money they had brought to pay for it back in the sacks. The nine brothers loaded up their donkeys and left. When they stopped for the night, they saw that their money was still in their sacks, and they were afraid. "Why is God doing this to us?" they asked.

The brothers returned home and told Jacob what Joseph had said, how they must return with Benjamin in order to free Simeon. "Absolutely not!" Jacob answered. "You want to take away Benjamin from me when I have already lost Joseph, and now Simeon, too? If anything happened to him, I would die." Reuben tried to convince Jacob to let Benjamin go, promising to be responsible for him, but Jacob still refused.

The famine continued to worsen, and it wasn't long before Jacob's family was out of food again. "Go to Egypt and buy us some more grain so we don't starve," Jacob said.

But his sons reminded him, "The ruler we spoke to gave us strict orders that we could not return without our youngest brother. We cannot go without Benjamin."

"Why did you tell him you had another brother?" Jacob asked. "Do you want to kill me with grief?"

"He asked us all sorts of questions about ourselves and our family," the brothers said. "We had no choice."

"I will take care of Benjamin," Judah promised. "I swear that I will bring him back to you safely."

It was clear they had no other option, so Jacob relented and said, "I pray that God will be with you when you stand before that ruler, and that you will be able to return with Benjamin as well as Simeon. But, if I lose my children, then I lose my children."

When the brothers arrived in Egypt, Joseph ordered his servants to prepare a feast for them. He asked, "How is your father? Is he still living?"

"Yes," the brothers answered. "He is alive and well."

Joseph went over to Benjamin and said, "And this must be the younger brother you told me about. God bless you, my son." After seeing his brother, Joseph was so overwhelmed with emotion that he had to leave the room and weep. When he came back, he said, "Serve the meal!"

Everyone sat down, and they realized that they had been seated in order from oldest to youngest. Joseph had also ordered his servants to give Benjamin five times as much food as everyone else.

After dinner, Joseph ordered his servants to fill the brothers' bags with grain and put their money back in their bags like before. He also had them put his silver cup in Benjamin's sack. Then he gave the bags back to the brothers and sent them on their way.

Before they had gotten far, Joseph's head servant rushed after them and said, "Is this how you repay my master's kindness? He was so good to you. Why would you steal his silver cup?"

"Sir," the brothers replied, "we are honest men. We have not stolen anything! Search our belongings. If you find anything that belongs to your master, the person who has it will be executed and the rest of us will be your slaves."

"No one needs to die," the servant said. "I will search your bags, but only the person who has stolen from my master will become his slave. The rest will be free to go."

The brothers unloaded their sacks, and the servant searched each one. He pulled the silver cup out of Benjamin's bag and said, "See! This is my master's silver cup. You have stolen from him!"

The brothers were so upset that they ripped their clothes in sorrow. They all went back to Joseph's house with Benjamin and the servant. When they arrived, Joseph said, "What have you done? Did you not think I would find out?"

Judah said, "Sir, how could we convince you that we are innocent? It appears God has decided we are guilty. You found the cup in our bags, so we will all be your slaves."

"I wouldn't punish all of you for one person's crime," Joseph said. "You are all free to go, except for the thief."

"Sir," Judah answered, "please let me stay as your slave instead. I swore an oath to our father that I would not let anything happen to Benjamin. If we were to return without him, our father would die of grief. Let me take his place."

When Joseph saw the way his brothers responded to this test, he was overcome with emotion again. "Everybody out!" he shouted, and all of his servants left. Then he spoke to his brothers in their own language. "It's me, Joseph," he said. "Is our father really still alive?" The brothers were too afraid to answer, but Joseph said, "Don't be afraid. Come closer. Yes, it is really me, your brother Joseph. You sold me into slavery, but don't blame yourselves. It was actually God who sent me here. He let all those things happen to me because He had a plan to save many lives, including yours. This famine has been going on for two years, and it will last another five. God showed me in advance that this would happen.

That is why Egypt has been able to save up so much food. What you meant for evil, God meant for good.

"Now, go. Tell our father about everything God has done for me here in Egypt. Then bring him and your families and come live with me here. I will ask Pharaoh to give you a place to live, and you will have plenty of food while we wait for the famine to end." Joseph gave his brother Benjamin a big hug, and all the brothers started crying.

Joseph hugged and kissed all of them. "I forgive you," he said. "I forgive you all."

Pharaoh agreed with Joseph's plan to bring his family to Egypt. He sent the brothers back with wagons and donkeys to carry their wives and children on the

long journey. When Jacob and his family arrived in Egypt, he rushed over to Joseph and gave him a big hug. "I didn't believe it at first," he said. "But it's true! You're alive, and I get to see you before I die!"

God used Joseph to save thousands of people from the famine, and all Joseph had to do was be faithful to love God and do what He said. God can use any situation for good, even when it seems impossible. Jacob's family would soon grow into a nation, and they would have a relationship with God. God was fulfilling His promise to Abraham, slowly but surely.

GOD USES MOSES TO SAVE HIS PEOPLE

EXODUS 1-14

Jacob and his family, the Israelites, lived in Egypt for a long time. They grew so numerous that the new Pharaoh was afraid of them. He didn't remember what Joseph had done for Egypt, so he made the Israelites his slaves to prevent them from threatening his power. He forced them to build cities and monuments for him, trying to crush them with hard labor. But God was with them, so the Israelites had more and more children and grew stronger and stronger.

Pharaoh ordered the midwives, the women who helped the Israelite women give birth, to kill any boy babies when they were born, but let the girls live. The midwives loved God and refused to obey Pharaoh. They told him, "The Israelite women are so strong and healthy that by the time we get there, the babies have already been born!"

Not to be stopped, Pharaoh ordered everyone to kill any baby boys born to the Israelites by throwing them into the Nile river. There was an Israelite woman named Jochebed who already had a son and a daughter, and she was pregnant with her third child. She decided that if her baby was a boy, she would protect him if she could.

When the baby came, it was a boy. Jochebed hid him for a while, but she knew she couldn't keep him hidden forever. She wove a little basket out of reeds, one that was just his size. Then she coated the basket with tar on the outside to make it waterproof. When she was done, she took her baby boy and the basket down to the Nile river. Her daughter, Miriam, was with her, and they put the baby in the basket and placed the basket in the reeds by the river's bank. They had found a way to keep him alive, but what would happen now? Miriam stood far off, to see what would be done to him.

The basket floated down the river and stopped among some rushes near the royal palace. That same time, the princess, one of Pharaoh's daughters, was coming down to the river to take a bath. While the princess was bathing, she saw the basket in the rushes, and sent a

53

servant to bring it to her. She opened the basket and smiled when she saw the baby inside. "This must be one of the Israelite babies," she said. "He's so cute! I will keep him and raise him as my own son."

Miriam climbed out of her hiding place and bowed to the princess. "Your Majesty," she said, "would you like me to find an Israelite woman to nurse this baby for you?"

"I would love that," the princess said. "Please find a woman who can nurse him and bring her to me."

Miriam ran home and told Jochebed what had happened then brought her to see the princess. Jochebed got to keep her son until he was weaned. When that day came, it was hard to say goodbye, but she was glad for the time she got to have with her baby. She brought him to the palace and gave him to the princess.

"I will call him Moses," the princess said, "because I took him out of the water."

Moses grew up in the palace. Life was good for him, but he knew that the rest of his people were suffering. When he was grown, Moses saw an Egyptian beating an Israelite slave. There was no one else around, so he hit the Egyptian so hard that he died. Moses buried the Egyptian's body in the sand and hoped no one had seen what he did.

The next day, Moses saw two Israelites arguing. "Don't fight," Moses said. "You're brothers, and brothers shouldn't fight."

"What are you going to do about it?" one of the men asked. "Are you going to kill me like that Egyptian?"

Moses was terrified. If these men knew what he had done, Pharaoh would know soon, too. He ran off into the desert so that Pharaoh wouldn't kill him.

In the desert, Moses met some women who were bringing their father's sheep to drink at a well. Some shepherds attacked the women, but Moses drove them off and helped the women get water. When the women brought Moses to meet their father, Jethro, he

invited Moses to stay with them. Moses married Jethro's daughter Zipporah and lived with his new family in the land of Midian.

While Moses was living in Midian, Pharaoh died. Pharaoh's son became the new Pharaoh. He continued to oppress the Israelites, and they cried out to God. One day, while Moses was watching his father in law's sheep, he saw something strange: A bush on a nearby mountain was on fire, but it wasn't burning up. Moses went over to investigate, but when he got close, a voice spoke to him from inside the burning bush.

"Moses," the voice said.

"Here I am," Moses said.

"Don't come any closer," the voice said. "Take off your sandals, because you are standing on holy ground. I am God, the God of your fathers, who appeared to Abraham, Isaac, and Jacob." Moses was afraid to look at God's presence in the bush, so he hid his face. "I have heard the cry of my people, the Israelites," God said. "I have seen how they are oppressed in the land of Egypt, so I am going to rescue them. I will bring them into a good land with plenty of food, the land of Canaan which I promised to give to Abraham and his descendants forever. Go to Pharaoh. I have chosen you to lead my people out of slavery and into the Promised Land."

"Who am I, oh Lord?" Moses asked. "I can't go before Pharaoh and lead your people."

"I will be with you," God promised. "When you lead the Israelites out of Egypt, you will bring them to this mountain, and they will worship me here."

"What if I tell the Israelites that the God of their ancestors has sent me and they ask me your name?" Moses asked. "What will I tell them?"

"I AM," God said. "I always have been and always will be the same. Tell them that YHWH, who is called 'I AM,' has sent you. That is my name, and they must use it for me forever. Go to the Israelite leaders and tell them that I have sent you to free them from Egypt. Then go to Pharaoh and tell him I have commanded you to bring the Israelites out into the desert to worship me. Pharaoh will not let you go unless I force him, so I will perform many miraculous signs and punish the Egyptians for mistreating my people. In the end, they will let you go, and they will even beg you to leave and give you gifts."

Moses was overwhelmed by what God was asking him to do. He said, "What if no one believes that you have sent me and they refuse to listen?"

God told Moses to throw down the walking stick in his hands. He did, and it became a snake. "Pick it up by the tail," God said. When Moses did, it turned back into a stick. Next, God told Moses to stick his hand into his cloak and pull it out again. When he did, it was covered in leprosy as white as snow. Then God told him to do it again. When he pulled his hand out the second time, the skin was normal.
"Perform these signs, and people will listen to you,"
God said. "They will know that I have sent you. If
they still don't believe, take some water from
the Nile and pour it on the ground; it will
become blood."

"I'm not good at speaking," Moses
said. "I talk slowly and don't
know what to say."

"Who made the mouth? Who causes it to speak?" God asked. "Don't you know that I made you? Go! When you speak, I will give you the words to say."

"Please, Lord," Moses said, "send someone else. I can't do it."

God was frustrated with Moses now. "Your brother, Aaron, is already coming out to find you," He said. "He will go with you and speak for you. You will tell him what I say, and he will tell your words to Pharaoh and the people. Go meet him, and bring your walking stick with you. I will use it to perform miracles."

Aaron met Moses, just like God had said, and the two of them went back to Egypt. They went to Pharaoh and said, "This is what the Lord God says: 'Let my people go out into the desert to worship me with sacrifices and hold a celebration.'"

Pharaoh said, "Who is this Lord, and why should I obey Him? I will not let the Israelites go. Why are you preventing my slaves from working? Everyone get back to work!"

The next day, Pharaoh ordered his overseers in charge of the Israelite slaves to no longer give the Israelites straw for making bricks, but the number of bricks they had to make stayed the same. The people

asked Moses and Aaron, "Why did you make Pharaoh angry? He is punishing us because of you, and now we hope that God will punish you, too."

Moses asked God why this was happening. God replied, "Don't worry. I will make it so that Pharaoh will let my people go. But first, I must work many wonders so that all who see it will know that I, the Lord, am the one who freed the Israelites from slavery. Then I will lead them into the land that I promised to Abraham, and the whole world will see that I keep my promises. I will be Israel's God, and they will be my people."

God sent Moses and Aaron back to Pharaoh, and said, "When he asks for a miraculous sign, throw your stick on the ground, and it will become a snake."

Moses and Aaron did what God told them, but Pharaoh wasn't impressed. He called his magicians and they were able to do the same thing. Aaron's snake ate the snakes of the magicians, but even then Pharaoh stubbornly refused to let the Israelites go.

"Because Pharaoh has been stubborn," God said, "I am going to bring plagues upon the land of Egypt to show my power. Tomorrow morning, go to Pharaoh again and tell him that if he does not let my people go, you will strike the Nile river with your stick and turn it to blood."

Moses and Aaron did what God said, and all the water in Egypt turned to blood. All the fish in the river died, and no one could drink any of the water. Even after this sign, Pharaoh still refused to let the Israelites go. His magicians did the same thing, turning water to blood with their secret arts, so Pharaoh remained stubborn.

A week later, Moses returned to Pharaoh with a new sign to perform. Pharaoh still refused to let the Israelites go, so Aaron held his stick over the river and frogs came up out of the water and covered the whole land. Pharaoh's magicians were able to do the same thing, but this time, Pharaoh said, "Okay, Moses, if you make these frogs go away, I will let your people go worship your God." So Moses prayed to God, and God made the frogs die until they only lived in the Nile. But when Pharaoh saw that the frogs were gone, he changed his mind and refused to let the Israelites go.

Next, God told Moses to have Aaron strike the ground with his stick. When he did, all the dust in Egypt turned into clouds of gnats. Pharaoh's magicians told him, "There is no way we can do anything like this. It must be God's doing." But Pharaoh was still stubborn and refused to let the Israelites go.

After this, God sent swarms of flies over the entire land of Egypt, except for Goshen, where the Israelites lived. Again, Pharaoh promised to let the Israelites go worship in the desert if Moses made the flies go away. Moses prayed, and God took the flies away. But Pharaoh changed his mind again and refused to let the Israelites go.

God sent more plagues on Egypt. He caused all the Egyptians' livestock to die, but none of the animals that belonged to the Israelites were harmed. He caused painful sores to break out on all the Egyptians and sent hailstones to destroy their crops and kill anyone who stayed outside in the storm. Then He sent swarms of locusts to eat up any plants that had survived the hail. After this, there was darkness that covered the entire land of Egypt, except for Goshen. After all this, Pharaoh still refused to let the Israelites go.

God had one last plague to bring upon the Egyptians, and it was the worst one. "Tell the people to get ready," God told Moses. "At midnight I am going to kill the firstborn son of every family in the land of Egypt, from Pharaoh's household to the lowest servant, no one will be spared. This is what the Israelites must do to protect themselves from my wrath: They must kill a lamb and use its blood to cover the doorposts of their homes. They must cook the lamb and eat it all with bread that has no yeast in it. Make sure you are wearing your traveling clothes, because after this, Pharaoh will send you out of Egypt once and for all. When the angel of my wrath sees the blood on your doorposts, it will pass over

your homes, but it will kill the firstborn son of every household that is not covered by the lamb's blood."

Moses warned Pharaoh and the Egyptians about what would happen, but Pharaoh refused to listen. At midnight, God did what He had said. He sent an angel to kill the firstborn son of every family who had not covered their doorposts with the blood of a lamb. All the firstborn sons in Egypt died, and everyone in the whole country wept and wailed, mourning for their sons.

Pharaoh summoned Moses and Aaron while it was still night and said, "Enough! Take your people and your livestock. Take anything you want and leave! Go worship your God. Please ask Him to be kind to me and stop all these punishments."

Moses and Aaron gathered all the people and set out into the desert. Their Egyptian neighbors gave them anything they wanted, showering them with valuables and supplies as they left. It had been exactly 430

years since Jacob's family first arrived in Egypt, and they were finally on their way back to Canaan, the Promised Land.

The people marched towards the Red Sea. When Pharaoh and his officials realized that they had lost their entire slave labor force, they got the army together and chased after the Israelites. The Israelites saw Pharaoh's army chasing after them with horses and chariots, and they were terrified. They said, "Moses! Did you bring us out here in the desert to die? We are trapped! The Egyptians will drive us into the sea and kill us!"

Moses prayed, and God said, "Don't be afraid of Pharaoh and his army. After today, you will never see any of them again. Stretch out your stick over the Red Sea." Moses did what God told him, and God sent a strong wind to blow on the water, making a path through the sea for the Israelites. They walked through the

Red Sea on dry ground. When all the Israelites were on the other side, Moses looked back and saw the Egyptian army following them through the sea. God said, "Stretch out your stick over the water again." When Moses did, the waters rushed back over the Egyptian army, killing all of them and their horses. Not a single soldier was left. God had rescued His people from Pharaoh and his army.

MEETING GOD IN THE DESERT

EXODUS 15-16; 19-34:9

After God saved the Israelites from the Egyptian army, Moses led them in a song of praise and thanksgiving to God. Now that they were safe, Moses had to bring the Israelites to the mountain where God had appeared to him in a burning bush. So, they set out into the desert toward Mount Sinai.

After traveling for three days, the Israelites finally found some water. But when they tasted the water, it was so bitter they couldn't drink it. The people complained to Moses that they had no water. Moses prayed, and God told him to throw a piece of wood in the water. When he did, it became safe to drink and the people stopped complaining.

The Israelites continued their journey through the desert, but the people complained again. They said, "We don't have any food; we are going to starve to death! Why did God bring us out of Egypt? At least there we had bread and meat to eat."

Moses asked God what to do about the lack of food. God told him what He would do, so Moses gathered all the Israelites together and Aaron said, "God has heard your complaints, and He will provide food for you. Every night you will have meat, and every morning you will have bread. You will know God is giving you this food because of the way He provides it."

That night, quails landed everywhere in the camp, so everyone who wanted could catch one to eat. The next morning, the ground was covered by thin flakes that stayed behind after the dew was gone. These flakes tasted sweet, like honey, and the people could collect the flakes

and make them into bread. Moses and Aaron told them, "God will provide this food every day, so only take as much as you need each day. Do not try to save any for tomorrow."

Some of the people didn't listen to Moses and took extra. The next day, the food they had saved was rotten and full of worms. After that, no one took more than they needed, and the leftovers evaporated in the sun.

Two months after they left Egypt, the Israelites arrived at Mount Sinai. They camped around the mountain, and Moses warned the people not to touch it. He told them to get ready and make themselves clean, because God was coming down to meet with them.

After three days, God appeared on the mountain, surrounded by thick clouds full of thunder and lightning. The clouds covered the whole mountain, and the Israelites were afraid of God's power. Moses went up on the mountain and talked with God. When God answered, it sounded like loud thunder.

God spoke out of the thunderclouds to all the Israelites. He said, "I am the Lord, your God, who brought you out of Egypt. Do not worship any gods besides me. Do not make any idols, and do not worship any idols. If you reject me and worship idols, I will punish you, but if you love and obey me, I will bless you and your descendants. Do not misuse my name. It is holy, and I will punish anyone who misuses it. Keep Saturday holy, a Sabbath day to honor me. You can work the other six days of the week, but do not work on the Sabbath, because that is the day that I rested from creating the world. Respect your parents. If you do, you will live a long, good life in the land I am giving you. Do not kill anyone. Be faithful

in marriage. Do not steal. Do not tell lies about others. Do not desire to take anything that belongs to others."

When the Israelites heard the voice of God, they were terrified. They told Moses, "Please, you go and talk to God for us, then tell us what He says. Don't let God speak to us or we will die!" So Moses kept talking to God, but the Israelites stayed far back from the mountain.

Moses came back and told the Israelites all the rules and commands God had for them, the rules for how to live with Him and be His people. All the Israelites promised, "We will do everything God has commanded us." Then Moses had Aaron and his sons build an altar, and they offered special sacrifices to set the people apart for God. Moses took some of the blood from the sacrifices and put it in a bowl. He took the blood and sprinkled it on the people, saying, "This blood is a sign of the promise that God is making with you today. You are His special people, and He will live with you and you will live with Him, obeying Him and loving Him and being loved by Him."

After sprinkling the people, Moses went back up on the mountain. When he had been on the mountain for a long time, the people started to think he had died. They had just promised to love God and follow His commands, but the Israelites decided to break God's first two rules. They asked Aaron to make an idol for them to worship, since Moses was gone. Aaron had all the people give him jewelry. He melted it down and made an image of a calf out of the gold. He said, "Look, Israel, this is your god, who brought you out of Egypt." The people worshiped the golden calf and threw a party to celebrate their new god.

God saw what the people were doing, and He sent Moses back down to them. God had carved the first ten commandments He gave Israel onto two stone tablets, and Moses was carrying them when he came off the mountain. He was so angry at what was happening in the camp that he smashed the tablets on the ground. He asked Aaron, "Why did you make this idol and cause the people to sin?"

"It's not my fault," Aaron said. "You know how much they like to sin. They thought you were dead, so they gave me their gold jewelry and asked me to make them a god. I threw the gold in the fire, and out came this calf!"

Moses called for anyone who was still on God's side, and the descendants of

Levi came over. He ordered them to
go kill the people who were worshiping the idol. When they had killed many idol
worshipers, Moses took the golden calf and ground
it up into powder, poured the powder into the water, and
made the rest of the people drink it.

God was so angry about what the Israelites had done that He
wanted to destroy them all, but He let Moses plead on their behalf,
reminding God of the promise He had made. God was merciful to the
Israelites and gave them a second chance. He made new stone tablets
and gave them to Moses so the people could always remember the
promise they had made to obey God and be His people, living
with Him and loving Him and being loved by Him.

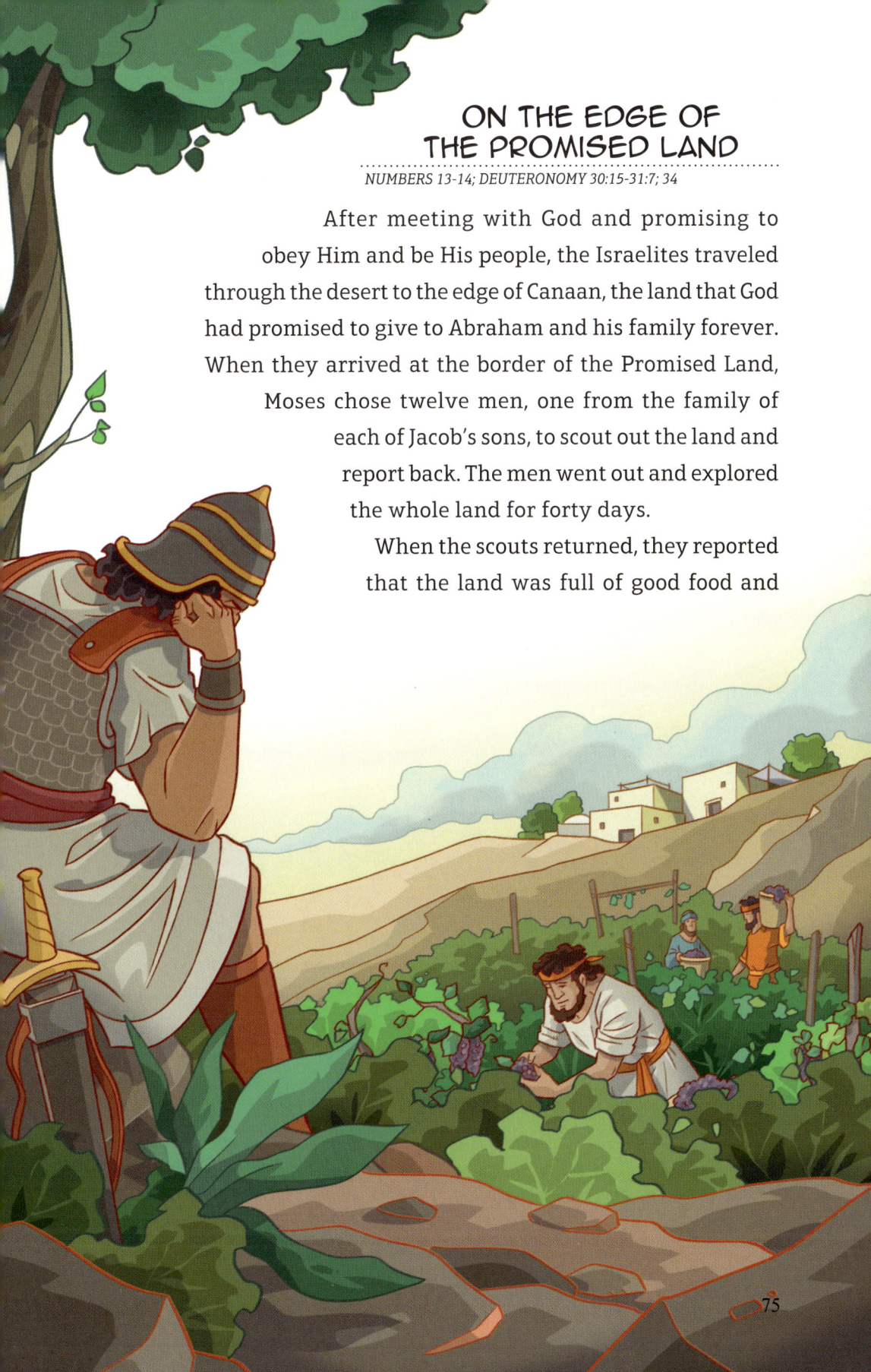

ON THE EDGE OF
THE PROMISED LAND

NUMBERS 13-14; DEUTERONOMY 30:15-31:7; 34

After meeting with God and promising to obey Him and be His people, the Israelites traveled through the desert to the edge of Canaan, the land that God had promised to give to Abraham and his family forever. When they arrived at the border of the Promised Land, Moses chose twelve men, one from the family of each of Jacob's sons, to scout out the land and report back. The men went out and explored the whole land for forty days.

When the scouts returned, they reported that the land was full of good food and plentiful fields. They even found a bunch of grapes that was so heavy it took two of them to carry it. They showed the people the fruit they had found, but then they said, "There are also giants living in the land, and they have strong, fortified cities. They are stronger than us—we look like grasshoppers compared to them!"

The people were afraid when they heard this, but two of the scouts, Caleb and Joshua, spoke up and said, "Don't be afraid! We can take the land, because God is with us. Let's go! God will give them into our hands."

The other scouts convinced the people not to listen to Joshua and Caleb, and they were too afraid to enter the land and fight the Canaanites, even though God had promised to lead them and give them victory. Some of the people even started talking about choosing a new leader and going back to Egypt. The people were threatening Moses and Aaron, but God suddenly appeared in a cloud over the tent where He met with them.

The Israelites backed off, and Moses went to the tent to talk with God. God was angry at the Israelites for their doubt and rebellion, so He said, "Moses, after all that I have done for these people, they still don't trust me. They reject me over and over. I want to destroy them."

"Please, Lord," Moses prayed, "don't destroy your people. What would the other nations think if you did that? They would think you destroyed them because you weren't powerful enough to give them the land you promised. Please continue to have mercy on us, like you have from the beginning."

"You're right," God told Moses. "I will continue to have mercy on Israel for the sake of my name and reputation. I will not destroy them all. But the ones who rebelled against me today, who refused to follow me into the Promised Land, will never see the land that I will give their children. They will all die in the

wilderness. Only Caleb and Joshua will live to see the Promised Land, because they trusted in me."

Because the people were too afraid to enter the Promised Land, Moses led them around the long way, through the desert and wilderness, for forty years. During that time, all the people who were twenty years old or older when the Israelites refused to enter the Promised Land died, except Joshua and Caleb. Moses' brother, Aaron, and his sister, Miriam, also died in the wilderness. By the time he led the people to the eastern edge of Canaan, near the Jordan river, Moses was very old. He knew he was going to die soon, so he gathered all the people together to remind them of their relationship with God.

Moses told the new generation of Israelites all the rules and commands that God had given to their parents, then he reminded them of how their parents had sinned by not trusting and following God. He told them, "I'm giving you two options today: life and death. If you obey all the words of the Law that God has given you, you will live a long time and be His people. But if you turn away from this Law and follow other gods, you will die like your parents did. Choose life! Follow God and take this land that He is giving you. Follow His laws and live with Him and love Him and be loved by Him in this land."

Then Moses called Joshua to join him. Joshua had been Moses' helper the whole time Israel was wandering in the wilderness, and Moses made Joshua the leader in his place. He told them all to follow Joshua like they had followed him, and he encouraged them all to be brave and strong and not to be afraid. He ordered them to follow God and obey Him for as long as they lived. Then, Moses went up on a nearby mountain and looked out over the Promised Land, the land that the Israelites were finally ready to enter, the land that God had promised to Abraham and Isaac and Jacob. Moses died there, old and full of years, having served God faithfully by leading His people and trusting in Him.

JOSHUA LEADS ISRAEL INTO THE PROMISED LAND

JOSHUA 1-3; 6

After Moses died, Joshua became the leader of Israel. God appeared to him and said, "I will be with you just like I was with Moses. No one will be able to defeat you. Now, go and cross the Jordan river and take over the land that I promised to give to your ancestor Abraham. Be brave and strong, and do not be afraid. Remember to read and obey the Law that Moses gave you, and I will be with you wherever you go, helping you take the Promised Land."

So, Joshua chose two men to be spies and scout out the first city in the Israelites' path, the city of Jericho. The two men went across the Jordan river and entered Jericho, where they stayed the night at the house of a woman named Rahab. Someone saw the spies enter the city, and they told the king of Jericho about it. When Rahab heard that the king's men were coming to look for the spies, she hid them under bundles of flax that she had put on her roof to dry. When the king's men came looking for the spies, she told them, "I saw those men, but they already left the city. If you hurry, you might catch them."

The soldiers left and went looking for the spies outside the city, and Rahab went up on the roof to tell the spies it was safe to leave. She said to the spies, "Everyone in the city is afraid of you Israelites because we have heard of the powerful signs your God has done, both in Egypt and in the wilderness. We know that your God is the One who made heaven and earth, and we are all afraid to fight against you. Please promise me in the name of your God that you will be kind to me and my family, like I have been kind to you. Please spare us when your God gives you the city."

The spies promised that Rahab and her family would be spared. They said, "When we come to conquer the city, hang a red cord out your window, so we know which house is yours. Then, gather all your family in your house, and do not leave your house at all. We will protect you and any of your family who are in your home."

Rahab's house was built into the wall of the city, so she was able to lower a rope for the spies to climb down and escape without being seen. The men hid until the soldiers had stopped looking for them, then they went back to Joshua and reported everything that had happened. "God has definitely given us this land," they told him. "All the people there are afraid of us." They also told him about Rahab and how she had helped them escape the city and the promise they had made to her.

Soon after, all the Israelites set out to cross the Jordan river into the Promised Land. Joshua had the priests carry the ark of the covenant, the special box that God had commanded them to build to hold the tablets with

the Law, in front of the people, representing the fact that God was leading His people. The river was flooding, but Joshua told the priests to step into the water and not be afraid. When they did, the water stopped flowing and piled up several miles upstream. The priests stood in the middle

of the riverbed until all of God's people had passed through, then they joined the rest on the other side. As soon as the last priest stepped out of the river, the water rushed back down, flooding it again.

Joshua had the people set up a pile of stones next to the river as a memorial of what God had done for them. He didn't want the Israelites to ever forget the power and provision of the God they served. After the monument was finished, the Israelites made camp near Jericho.

Now, Jericho had thick walls that would take a long time to break through. They were so thick that there were houses in the wall, like Rahab's, and no one had ever broken them down. All the people of Jericho were afraid of Israel, so they had locked the gates and refused to open them or leave their homes. Joshua was trying to come up with a plan to attack the city, when God spoke to him. "I will help you defeat the king of Jericho," God said. "Here's what you need to do: March around the city once a day for six days. Have the priests carry the ark of the

covenant and seven trumpets in front of the people. On the seventh day, march around the city seven times while the priests blow the trumpets. Then, after the seventh time around, have the priests blow a loud blast and have all the people shout. The walls of Jericho will come tumbling down and you will be able to attack it from all sides.

Joshua ordered the people to do what God had told him. For six days, they marched out to Jericho and marched slowly around the city once before going back to their camp. They carried the ark of the covenant in front of them, but Joshua had ordered them not to make a noise until he commanded them to shout. On the seventh day, they marched around seven times, and the priests were blowing their trumpets. "Get ready to shout," Joshua said. "The walls will come down, and we will destroy everything in the city to show that it belongs to God. Do not leave anyone alive except for Rahab and the people in her house, and destroy everything. Do not take anything from the city. It all belongs to God."

The priests blew a loud blast on their trumpets, and all the people shouted at the top of their lungs. The thick walls of Jericho that the inhabitants had thought they could hide behind came crumbling and tumbling down. The Israelites gave another shout and rushed in from all sides, taking the city by force and destroying everything in it. Joshua called the two spies over and ordered them to find Rahab and bring her and her family out safely. When Rahab was safely out of the city, the people set it on fire and destroyed it completely.

Jericho was only the first city of many. Joshua led God's people to victory all over the Promised Land, and they followed God, obeying Him and loving Him for as long as Joshua lived. At last, God's promise to Abraham had been fulfilled. The Israelites were living in the Promised Land, and they were God's chosen people, living in a relationship with Him. They followed the rules that He gave them, and they were able to live with Him in a way that had not been possible since sin entered the world.

DEBORAH, THE WISE

JUDGES 2:8-4:22

After Joshua died, the people forgot about their promise to God. They stopped worshiping Him and started worshiping the idols of the Canaanites instead. They worshiped false gods named Baal and Ashtoreth, and many other idols. Because of their sin against Him, God sent the surrounding nations to conquer Israel. These nations oppressed the Israelites and treated them badly. Eventually, the people remembered God and cried out to Him, asking Him to forgive and rescue them. When they did this, God chose people to be heroes and rulers. These heroes were called judges, and as long as they lived, the people followed God, but when they died, the people went right back to worshiping idols.

One of the times Israel sinned against God by worshiping idols, God let a Canaanite army led by a man named Sisera conquer them. Sisera and his army made life miserable for Israel for twenty years. Finally, they asked God to forgive and rescue them. When they did, God spoke to a wise woman named Deborah. God gave Deborah a message for a man named Barak, so she sent word for him to come meet her.

When Barak arrived, Deborah told him, "I have a message from God for you! Gather an army of ten thousand men and go to Mount Tabor. God will trick Sisera into fighting you, and He will help you defeat Sisera and his army."

Barak wasn't so sure about this idea, so he said, "I will only go if you come with me."

"That's fine," Deborah said. "I'll come with you. But, since you were afraid to go without my help, then God will make sure a woman kills Sisera, and you will not get any credit for the victory."

Barak and Deborah gathered an army of Israelites and assembled at Mount Tabor. When they got there, Sisera and his army were getting ready to fight. "Go, Barak," Deborah said. "Go and fight against Sisera! God is with you, and He will fight for you and give you victory!" Barak and his ten thousand soldiers fought against Sisera and his army, and God confused Sisera's army so that they couldn't fight because they were so afraid of Barak and the Israelites. The entire enemy army was destroyed, and only Sisera escaped.

Sisera ran from the Israelite army, and he came to a man named Heber and his wife Jael. Sisera went to Jael's tent and asked for a drink of water. "Come in, sir," Jael said. Sisera went in and sat down. Jael poured him a glass of milk to drink and gave him a blanket so he could rest while she kept watch. When Sisera was asleep, Jael took a hammer and a tent peg and crept over to him. Jael took the hammer and drove the tent peg through one side of Sisera's skull and out the other, into the ground.

When the army came looking for Sisera, Jael told Barak, "The man you are looking for is inside my tent. Come and see." Barak followed her, and there was Sisera, dead on the ground. God had rescued His people, and His promise to Deborah came true. This was not the first time the Israelites turned from God, then repented, and it would not be the last. He rescued them each time, because even when people are not faithful, God still is. He made a promise to be Israel's God and to rescue them when they turned to Him, and He always keeps His promises.

GIDEON'S UNLIKELY VICTORY
JUDGES 6-8

Another time the Israelites turned away from God, He sent the nation of Midian to punish them. The Midianites raided the Israelites, killing and stealing and burning their crops, making it hard for them to live. When the people cried out to God for forgiveness and help, God chose an unlikely hero to save them, a man named Gideon.

Gideon was in the bottom of a wide pit that was normally used to crush grapes for making wine. He was threshing his wheat at the bottom of the pit, beating it with a heavy stick to separate the edible grains from the stalk and chaff. He was doing this because he was afraid the Midianites might see him and come steal his food. While Gideon was threshing his grain in this unusual place, an angel appeared to him from God. "The Lord is with you, mighty warrior," the angel told Gideon.

Gideon was confused, so he said, "No offense, but if God is with us, then why are all these bad things happening to us?"

Then God spoke through the angel and said, "I will be with you, Gideon. I will make you strong, and you will defeat the Midianites."

Gideon still wasn't sure, so he asked the angel to wait until he brought an offering for God. He went and got some food and put it on a stone in front of the angel. The angel touched the food with his walking stick and it burst into flames, then the angel disappeared. That night, God spoke to Gideon again. "Go take your father's seven-year-old bull and use it to tear down the shrine to Baal and the Canaanite gods," God said. "Then build an altar to me and offer the bull as a sacrifice on it."

Gideon did what God told him to do, and in the morning, the shrine to Baal was torn down and he had offered the bull as a sacrifice to God on a new altar. The people of the town wanted to kill Gideon for what he did, but Gideon's father said, "If Baal is angry about what he did, let Baal take revenge on him. If he really is a god, he should be able to defend his own altar."

After this, Gideon went out and gathered an army of Israelites to fight against the army of Midian. The army gathered near a spring, and God said to Gideon, "Your army is too big. If I let you defeat Midian with this army, the Israelites will think that they saved themselves and I had nothing to do with it. I want you to tell everyone who is afraid to fight that they can go home." Gideon told the soldiers that if anyone was afraid to fight, they could go home, and two thirds of his army left.

"That's still too many soldiers," God said. "Take the men down to the stream and have them drink from it. Divide them into groups based on how they drink, whether they kneel down to drink or scoop up water in their hands." Gideon obeyed, and there were three hundred men who scooped up water with their hands. The rest knelt down to drink. God said, "Your army will be just the men who scooped up water with their hands. Send everyone else home. I am going to rescue Israel from Midian with only three hundred men."

Gideon took his army of three hundred soldiers and camped on a hill near the Midianite army. That night, God said, "Get up, Gideon. Attack the Midianite army, and I will give you victory over them. If you are still afraid, sneak down to their camp and listen to what they are saying about you."

Gideon and his servant sneaked down to the Midianite camp until they could hear some guards talking. The camp was so big that it seemed like there must be more

Midianite soldiers than grains of sand on a beach. "I had a dream last night," one of the guards said. "In my dream, a loaf of barley bread rolled into the camp and hit a tent. When it did, the tent flipped over and collapsed."

"Your dream must be about Gideon, the Israelite leader," the other guard said. "It means that God will let him and his army defeat our entire army."

When Gideon heard this, he praised God and hurried back to the Israelite camp. "Let's go!" he said. "God is going to help us defeat the Midianites."

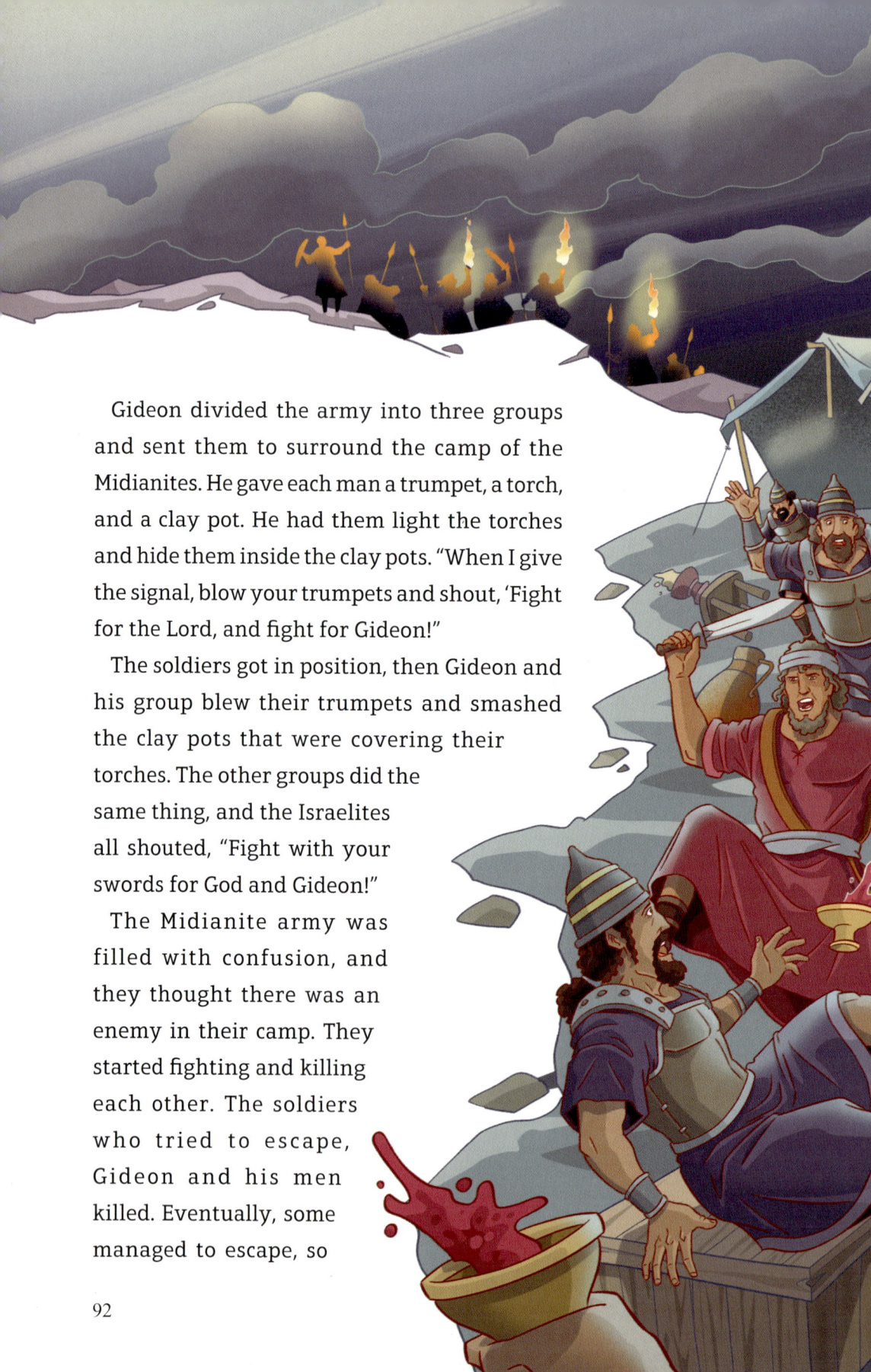

Gideon divided the army into three groups and sent them to surround the camp of the Midianites. He gave each man a trumpet, a torch, and a clay pot. He had them light the torches and hide them inside the clay pots. "When I give the signal, blow your trumpets and shout, 'Fight for the Lord, and fight for Gideon!'

The soldiers got in position, then Gideon and his group blew their trumpets and smashed the clay pots that were covering their torches. The other groups did the same thing, and the Israelites all shouted, "Fight with your swords for God and Gideon!"

The Midianite army was filled with confusion, and they thought there was an enemy in their camp. They started fighting and killing each other. The soldiers who tried to escape, Gideon and his men killed. Eventually, some managed to escape, so

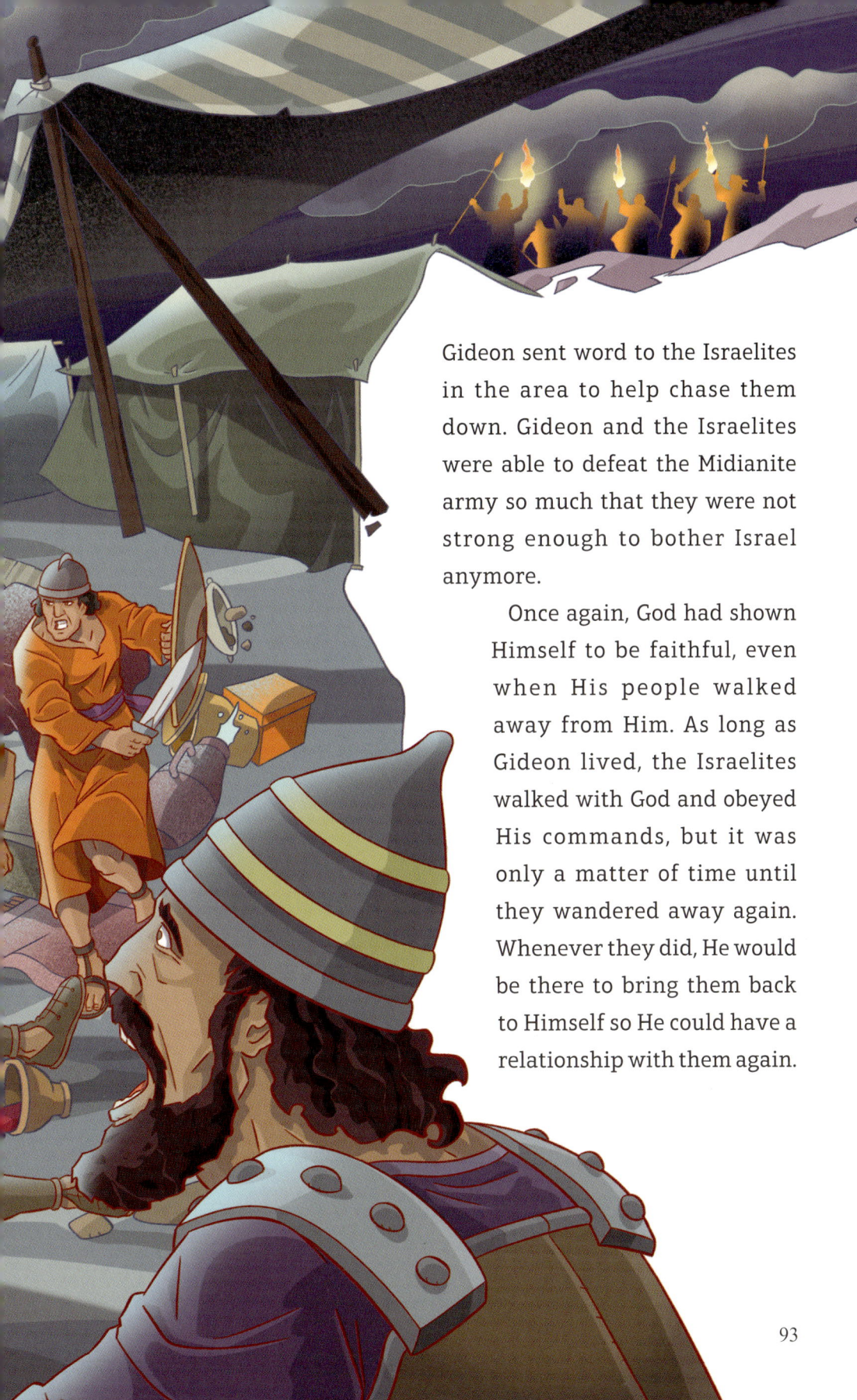

Gideon sent word to the Israelites in the area to help chase them down. Gideon and the Israelites were able to defeat the Midianite army so much that they were not strong enough to bother Israel anymore.

Once again, God had shown Himself to be faithful, even when His people walked away from Him. As long as Gideon lived, the Israelites walked with God and obeyed His commands, but it was only a matter of time until they wandered away again. Whenever they did, He would be there to bring them back to Himself so He could have a relationship with them again.

THE STRONGEST MAN WHO EVER LIVED

JUDGES 13-14; 16

Israel rebelled against God and worshiped idols again, so He let the Philistines rule over them. The people called out to God for help and forgiveness yet again, so God spoke to a man named Manoah and his wife. God said, "Even though you haven't been able to have any children, you will soon have a son. He is going to belong to me. He must never cut his hair or drink alcohol or eat anything forbidden by the Law. I will use him to rescue my people from the Philistines."

Manoah and his wife had a son, just like God said, and they named him Samson. They never cut his hair, and they obeyed everything God had told them. God was with Samson and blessed him. When he was grown, God's Spirit came down on Samson and gave him supernatural strength.

One day, Samson saw a young woman in the Philistine town of Timnah. "I must marry her," Samson told his parents. "Get her for me."

"Why would you want to marry a Philistine?" his parents asked. "Marry an Israelite woman instead."

"I like her," Samson said. "Get her for me!"

Samson and his parents set out for Timnah. Samson was walking by himself when a lion came up and attacked him. God's Spirit filled Samson with power, and he ripped the lion apart with his bare hands. Samson returned to his parents, but he didn't tell them about the lion. When they arrived in Timnah, the young woman's father agreed to the marriage, so Samson and his parents returned home to prepare for the wedding.

On the way back for the wedding, Samson found the corpse of the lion where it had attacked him before. Some wild bees had built a hive inside it, so Samson scooped out some of the honey and ate it. He brought some to his parents too, but he didn't tell them where he had gotten it.

Samson threw a weeklong wedding celebration, and on the first day he made a bet with thirty young men. He said, "I will tell you a riddle. If you cannot guess the answer by the end of the week, you each will give me a new set of clothes. But, if you can guess the answer, I will give

each of you a new set of clothes." The young men agreed, so Samson told them his riddle, "Out of the strong comes something sweet. Out of the eater comes something to eat."

The young men tried to figure out Samson's riddle all week, but they couldn't guess the answer. On the last day of the celebration, they went to his bride and said, "If you don't trick your husband into telling you the answer to his riddle, we will burn your whole family to death."

Samson's bride begged him to tell her the answer, and after she had pestered him over and over, he told her about the honey from the lion. Once she knew the answer, the young woman told the young men. They came to Samson and said, "What is stronger than a lion? What is sweeter than honey?"

Samson knew that his bride must have told them the answer, and he was angry. He went to a nearby town, killed thirty Philistine men, and took their clothes to give to the young men.

Samson then stormed home, leaving his bride behind. When he saw that Samson had left her there, the young woman's father arranged for her to marry one of the young men instead.

Later on, Samson fell in love with another Philistine woman named Delilah. The Philistine leaders were angry with Samson for killing many of their people and causing trouble for them. They told Delilah, "If you can trick Samson into revealing the secret of his incredible strength so we can capture him, we will make you rich."

The next time Samson visited Delilah, she asked him, "Samson, how did you get so strong? How could I tie you up so you can't escape? If you tell me, I promise I won't tell."

"Okay," Samson told her. "If you tie me up with seven new bowstrings, I will be as weak as anyone else."

Delilah believed Samson. When he fell asleep, she tied him up with seven new bowstrings, then she shouted, "Samson, look out! The Philistines are attacking!" Samson sat up and ripped the bowstrings apart like they were nothing.

Samson told Delilah more lies about how to tie him up, and each time, he woke up and broke the ropes she used. "You keep lying to me," Delilah said. "Tell me the truth. How can I really tie you up?" She kept bothering Samson until he couldn't take it anymore. One day, he told her the truth.

"Ever since I was born," he said, "I have belonged to God. I have never once cut my hair, because it is the symbol that I am God's. If my hair was ever cut, then God's power would leave me and I would be as weak as anyone else."

Delilah knew Samson had told her the truth this time, so she told the Philistine leaders to get ready. When Samson fell asleep, she cut off all his hair. By the time she was finished, he was as weak an ordinary man. Then Delilah shouted, "Samson, look out! The Philistines are attacking!"

Samson sat up, expecting to break free like every other time, but he was trapped. His hair was gone, and so was his strength. The Philistines chained him up and poked out his eyes. They took him to their capital city and made him push a huge millstone. While he was in prison, Samson's hair began to grow back.

The rulers of the Philistines threw a big party in the temple of their god Dagon. They sacrificed many animals and had a huge feast. One of them said, "Since we finally captured Samson, let's bring him out so we can praise Dagon for giving us victory." The Philistines brought Samson to the temple. They put him near a support pillar so he could lean on it.

The people mocked Samson, saying, "Look at him! He used to destroy our people, but now he is weak and pitiful!"

Samson realized that he was standing next to the two main pillars that held up the roof. He heard how big the crowd of Philistines in the temple was, so he prayed quietly under his breath, "God, please remember me and give me strength one last time so I can get revenge on these Philistines." He grabbed the support pillars and said, "Let me die with the Philistines!" God's Spirit gave Samson strength one final time, and when he pushed on the pillars, they toppled down, collapsing the entire temple and killing all the Philistines inside. Samson killed even more Philistines when he died than he had during his life.

God used even a selfish, angry person like Samson to save His people. God will use anyone who listens to Him and loves Him and wants to live with Him. Even when we are weak and frail, God is strong, and He gives us His power.

WHEREVER YOU GO, I WILL GO

THE BOOK OF RUTH

During the time when judges ruled Israel, an Israelite named Elimelech moved from Bethlehem to Moab with his wife Naomi and their two sons. While they were there, Elimelech died, leaving Naomi a widow. When Naomi's sons grew up, they married two women from Moab, named Orpah and Ruth. Soon after, both of Naomi's sons died, leaving her with no one to take care of her. Naomi decided to return to Bethlehem on her own.

"We want to go with you," Orpah and Ruth told Naomi.

"No, my daughters," Naomi said, "You should go home to your own people. I have nothing to offer you. I can't even provide for myself."

Orpah hugged and kissed Naomi and cried, but she eventually left and returned to her family. Naomi told Ruth, "Your sister-in-law is going back to her people. Don't you want to go with her?"

"Don't make me leave you!" Ruth said. "Wherever you go, I will go, and wherever you stay, I will stay. Your God will be my God, and your people will be my people."

When Naomi saw that Ruth would not leave, she stopped trying to convince her. She was grateful that Ruth loved her enough to stay, even though the future didn't look very bright for them. The two women went to Bethlehem, and the townspeople were glad to see Naomi again.

It was harvest season, so Ruth told Naomi, "I'll go out into the fields and see if I can find some harvesters who will let me gather the grain they leave behind." She went out and found a field that belonged to a man named Boaz. Boaz was an important man in Bethlehem, and he was related to Elimelech, Naomi's husband.

When Boaz came to check on his workers, he asked them, "Who is that young woman gathering grain behind you?"

"She's the Moabite woman who came back with Naomi," the workers answered.

Boaz went over to Ruth and said, "I don't want you to go to any other fields to gather grain. Stay here in my field and gather as much as you

want with the women who work for me. I've told the men not to bother you, and to let you have water from their jars whenever you want."

"Why are you being so nice to me?" Ruth asked. "I'm just a foreigner."

"I've heard about how you helped Naomi ever since your husband died. You even left your own family and country to come here with her and help provide for her in an unfamiliar land. I hope the God of Israel blesses you and rewards you for what you have done."

Ruth worked the rest of the day and brought home a big basket of grain to show Naomi. When Naomi saw how much Ruth had gathered, she said, "God bless the man who treated you so well and let you gather so much! Where did you work today? Whose field was it?"

"A man named Boaz owns the field," Ruth said, "and he asked me to keep coming back until the harvest is over."

"May God bless Boaz!" Naomi said. "He is one of our close relatives who is supposed to take care us. He is still loyal to his family, even though Elimelech is dead."

After the harvest, Naomi told her, "I think it's time to find you a new husband who can provide for you. And I have a good idea of who it should be. You've been working in Boaz's field, and you know he is a relative of my husband's who is supposed to take care of us. Here's what you should do: Take a bath and put on nice smelling perfume and your best dress. Go out to the threshing floor where Boaz is working, but don't let him see you. When he is asleep, lift up the blanket over his feet and lie down under the corner of the blanket. Then see what he says."

Ruth did what Naomi said. When Ruth had lain down under the corner of Boaz's blanket, he woke up and said, "Who's there?"

"It's me, Ruth," she answered. "You are a relative who is supposed to take care of me, so please marry me if you are willing."

"May God bless you, Ruth!" Boaz said. "Coming to me shows how faithful you are to your family. You could have looked for a younger man, but you came to me, the one who is supposed to take care of you. I would be happy to marry you. Everyone in town knows how wonderful you are."

Boaz went out the next day and made the arrangements to marry Ruth. After they were married, they had a son named Obed. Obed would be the grandfather of an important person in Israel's history: King David. Because Ruth loved Naomi and wanted to become part of her people, God blessed her and gave her a loving husband and a new family. God loves to use relationships to bless people who love and obey Him. Through Ruth's relationship with Naomi, she was able to become a part of God's people and have a relationship with Him, which is the greatest relationship of all.

SAMUEL LISTENS TO GOD

1 SAMUEL 1; 2:18-21; 3 -4

A man named Elkanah lived during the time of the judges. He had two wives named Hannah and Peninnah. Peninnah had several children, but Hannah had none. Every year, Elkanah's family went to Shiloh, the place where the God's house was. The priest in charge of God's house was named Eli, and he had two sons, Hophni and Phinehas, who were also priests. When Elkanah's family came to worship God in Shiloh, they offered an animal as a sacrifice and ate the meat. Elkanah gave Peninnah and her children one piece each, but he gave Hannah two pieces because he loved her the most.

Peninnah always mocked Hannah and treated her badly because she didn't have any children. One time, when they were in Shiloh, Hannah was so upset that she cried and cried and couldn't eat. Elkanah tried to cheer Hannah up, but it didn't work. While the rest of the family were eating, Hannah went to God's house. Eli was sitting by the door and saw her go in. Hannah was so sad that she was weeping uncontrollably and shaking as she prayed. She said, "Lord God, you can do anything. I am your servant, and I am miserable beyond belief! Please give me a son. If you do, I will give him to you, and I will never cut his hair as a sign that he belongs to you."

Hannah was so upset that she couldn't even speak out loud. She prayed in her heart, and her mouth moved silently. Eli saw her shaking and moving her mouth, and he thought she was drunk. He said, "Are you really going to worship God drunk? Go sober up, then come back."

"Please, sir," Hanna said, "don't think that I am being disrespectful. I am not drunk, and I haven't been drinking. I'm just so miserable and upset. I have been praying to God and telling Him my problems."

Eli saw that she was not drunk, and he said, "Then you may go home and rest easy. I'm sure God has heard your prayer and will answer it."

"Thank you for being so kind to me, sir," Hannah said. She went back to her family, and she already felt much better.

Later, God answered Hannah's prayer by blessing her and Elkanah with a son. She named him Samuel, and when the time came to go to Shiloh, she said, "I'll stay here with Samuel until he is able to eat solid food. Then I will bring him to Shiloh and he will live there, serving the Lord for the rest of his life."

When Samuel was old enough, Hannah brought him to Shiloh. Elkanah offered his offering, and Hannah brought Samuel to Eli. "Sir," she said, "I was here a few years ago, praying to God. I asked the Lord to bless me with a child, and now here he is! God blessed me and gave me what I asked for, so now I am giving him back to God, to serve Him for as long as he lives."

Samuel stayed with Eli in Shiloh and lived at God's house. Hannah made him clothes every year and brought them along when Elkanah's family came to worship God. When they came, Eli blessed them, saying, "God gave you Samuel in answer to your prayers. Now I pray that God blesses you with even more children." Sure enough, Hannah and Elkanah had three more boys and two girls. But Samuel kept living with Eli at God's house.

God didn't speak to many people in those days, but one night, while Samuel and Eli were asleep, God called to Samuel.

Samuel got up and ran to Eli's room. "Here I am," he said. "What do you want?"

"I didn't call you," Eli said. "Go back to sleep."

Then God called Samuel's name a second time.

"Here I am," Samuel said, going back to Eli. "What do you need?"

"Son," Eli said, "I didn't call you. Go back to bed."

Samuel had never heard God speak before, so he didn't realize who was calling him. God

called him a third time, and he went back to Eli again. "Here I am," he said. "What do you want?"

This time, Eli realized that God was calling Samuel. He said, "Go back and lie down. If you hear the voice again, say, 'Speak, Lord. I am your servant, and I am listening.'"

Samuel went back, and God called him again, "Samuel! Samuel!"

"Yes, Lord," Samuel said. "I am your servant, and I am listening."

"I'm going to do something that will surprise everyone in Israel," God said. "I'm telling you because I want you to be my prophet. When I do what I am telling you, everyone will know that I have spoken to you. I will punish Eli and his family because his sons are wicked and he has done nothing to stop them. He lets them disrespect me and mistreat my people, so they will all die on the same day."

The next morning, Eli asked Samuel what God had told him. "Tell me everything," he said, "even if it's bad." So Samuel told Eli what God had said about his family. Eli replied, "The Lord is God. He will do what is right."

Later, what God told Samuel came true. Eli and his sons died on the same day, and everyone knew that God had spoken through Samuel. From then on, God spoke to Samuel and told him what to do. Samuel led the people as a judge and a prophet, helping them know how to live with God as His people, how to love Him and obey Him and have a relationship with Him.

ISRAEL'S FIRST KING
1 SAMUEL 8; 9:24-10:25

Samuel was getting older, and his sons were not good leaders like he was, so the Israelites got together and said, "We want a king, just like the other nations have. Choose one for us!"

Samuel didn't like this idea, so he asked God what to do. "Do whatever they say," God answered. "It's not you they have rejected as their leader, it's me. Give them the king they want."

Now, there was a man from the tribe of Benjamin named Kish. Kish was rich, and his son Saul was tall and handsome. One day, some of Kish's donkeys ran away, so Saul took a servant with him and went looking for them. Saul and the servant were gone for several days, and Saul said, "Let's go back. We've been gone so long that my father is probably more worried about us than the donkeys."

"Wait a little longer," the servant said. "I've heard a prophet lives nearby. Let's go ask him where the donkeys are."

So, Saul and the servant went to Samuel's town, and they met him in the gate. Saul said, "Sir, can you tell us where the prophet is? We heard that he sees visions, and we have come to talk to him."

"I am the prophet," Samuel said. "I'm on my way to the place of worship. Come along and eat dinner with me, then I will answer your questions in the morning. Don't worry about your missing donkeys. They're already back home."

Samuel took Saul and the servant to the place of worship and gave them dinner and let them stay with him. In the morning, Samuel said, "It's time for you to go back home. Have your servant go ahead of you a little." When they were alone, Samuel took out some olive oil and poured it on Saul's head. Samuel kissed Saul's forehead and told him, "God has chosen you to be Israel's king. From now on, every valuable thing in Israel will belong to you and your family."

Saul went home, but he didn't tell anyone what Samuel had told him. When the time came for Samuel to announce who would be the king, he gathered everyone in a town called Mizpah. He said, "God was the one who rescued you from Egypt and led you through the wilderness to this Promised Land. He has constantly rescued you from your enemies, but now you have rejected Him as your ruler. You said, 'We want a king to rule us like the other nations.' So, send forward representatives from every tribe and family clan so God can choose your king."

Samuel brought the representatives of each tribe in front of the altar, one at a time, and cast lots to see whom God would choose.

God chose the tribe of Benjamin. Then Samuel brought the representatives of each family clan from the tribe of Benjamin forward one at a time, and God chose Saul's family clan. Finally, God chose Saul out of his whole family, but no one knew where he was. The people prayed, "Is Saul here?"

"Yes," God answered. "He is hiding behind the baggage."

The people went and got Saul from behind the baggage and brought him in front of everyone. Samuel said, "Look at the man God has chosen to be your king. There is no one else like him!"

Everyone shouted, "Long live the king!"

Samuel explained to Saul what his duties would be as king of God's people and wrote them all down for him in a book. It was Saul's job to lead God's people, to protect them and set a good example for them when it came to loving God and obeying Him. It was a big, scary responsibility, but Saul was ready to take it on.

DAVID, THE FUTURE KING
1 SAMUEL 15:10-17:52

King Saul started well, but he soon stopped obeying God and started doing things his own way. One day, God told Samuel, "Saul will not be king much longer. He always disobeys me, so I have chosen someone else. Take some olive oil and visit a man in Bethlehem named Jesse. I have chosen one of his sons to be the next king."

Samuel obeyed God and traveled to Bethlehem. When he got to Jesse's house, Jesse introduced Samuel to his sons. When Samuel saw Eliab, the oldest, he thought, This must be the one God has chosen. He's so tall and strong.

"Don't judge by his looks," God told Samuel. "I haven't chosen him to be king. I don't judge the way people judge. People only look at the outside, but I look at the heart."

The second oldest came out to meet Samuel, but Samuel said, "God has not chosen him either."

Seven of Jesse's sons all came to meet Samuel, but God had not chosen any of them. Finally, Samuel said, "Do you have any other sons?"

"Well," Jesse said, "there's the youngest, David. He's watching the sheep."

"Send for him," Samuel said.

When David arrived, God told Samuel, "He's the one. Pour oil on his head as a sign that I have chosen him."

Samuel got up and poured oil on David's head in front of everyone. From then on, God's Spirit was with David. Samuel went back home; his job was finished.

God's Spirit had left Saul, and an evil spirit was bothering him, making him afraid. His advisors said, "Let's find someone who is gifted at playing the harp and have them come to the palace. When the evil spirit bothers you, they can play beautiful music for you until you feel better."

"Good idea," Saul said. "Let's do it."

"One of Jesse's sons is a talented musician," one of the advisors said. "He's also brave, handsome, and a good speaker."

Saul sent a message to Jesse and said, "Please send David to live in my palace and play the harp for me."

David left home and went to work for King Saul. Saul sent a letter back to Jesse and said, "Please let David stay here with me. I really like him and his music." Whenever Saul was upset because of the evil spirit, David would play the harp for him until the spirit left and he felt better.

During Saul's reign, the Philistines were constantly at war with Israel. Once, when the Israelite army was camped across a valley from the Philistine army, a giant came down into the valley from the Philistine side. His name was Goliath, and he was over nine feet tall. He was so big and strong that he had special armor and weapons that had been made just for him. Goliath came down into the valley twice a day, and he mocked the Israelites.

"Why are you lining up to fight?" Goliath asked. "Just choose one man to be your champion and send him to fight me. If he can beat me in single combat, we will be your slaves. But if I beat him, you will be our slaves. There must be someone in your army brave enough to fight me! Send me a challenger!"

Saul and his army heard Goliath's challenge, but they were all terrified. No one was brave enough to face the giant. Goliath challenged the Israelites like this for forty days, and Saul's entire army was afraid of him.

David's older brothers were serving in the army, so Jesse gave David some bread and roasted grain to bring them, and sent him to their camp. When he got there, the soldiers were getting into battle positions, so David left the food with the person in charge of the supplies and hurried to find his brothers. He asked them how they were, then Goliath came out to give his daily challenge.

The soldiers were afraid and started talking. "He keeps coming out to mock us," they said. "The king is offering a reward to anyone that can kill him. Whoever does it will get to marry the king's daughter, and his whole family will never have to pay taxes again."

"Is that true?" David asked one of the soldiers nearby. "Who does this Philistine think he is, anyway? He is insulting our people and mocking the armies of the living God!"

The soldiers told Saul what David said, and he sent for David. When David arrived in the king's tent, he said, "Your Majesty, we can't let this Philistine make us into cowards! I'll go fight him myself for daring to insult God's people."

"You wouldn't stand a chance," Saul said. "You're just a young man, and he's an experienced soldier who has been training his whole life."

"Your Majesty," David answered, "I am a shepherd; it's my job to watch over my father's sheep. If one of them is dragged off by a lion or a bear, I go after it and beat the wild animal until it lets them go. I've killed both lions and bears like this, and this Philistine will be just like one of them. He should not have insulted the army of the living God!"

"Okay," Saul said. "Go ahead and fight him. I hope that God helps you."

Saul ordered his own armor and weapons for David, but they were too big for him. Instead, he grabbed his shepherd's staff, went to a nearby stream, and put five smooth stones in his pouch.

Then he took out his sling and marched down into the valley to fight Goliath.

When Goliath saw that David was just a young man, he laughed and said, "Am I a dog? Is that why you're coming to fight me with a stick? When I'm done with you, I will feed your corpse to the wild animals."

David didn't back down. He replied, "You come against me with a sword and a spear, but I come against you in the name of the Lord Almighty,

the God of Israel, whom you have mocked and insulted."

David ran toward the giant and took a stone from his pouch, putting it into his sling. He swung the sling around and let the rock fly. The stone soared through the air and hit Goliath in the forehead, cracking his skull. Goliath fell down with a crash and didn't get up again. David took Goliath's own sword and used it to cut off the giant's head. He had defeated Goliath with just a sling and a stone, because God was on his side. When the Philistines saw what had happened to their champion, they panicked and ran. The Israelite army chased after them and defeated them. This was just the beginning of what God would do through David, His chosen king.

SAUL HUNTS DAVID

1 SAMUEL 18:1-20:41; 24

Soon, everyone was singing songs about David's victory over Goliath. They sang, "Saul has killed a thousand enemies, but David has killed ten thousand!"

Saul heard this song and said, "They love David more than me. They'll want to make him king next!" Saul was so jealous of David that he wanted to kill him. Once, while David was playing the harp for Saul, Saul took a spear and threw it at David. David quickly dodged out of the way, and the spear stuck in the wall.

Saul decided to put David in charge of his armies, both to get him away from the palace, and to put him in danger. He was afraid of David because he knew that God was helping David, but had left him because of his disobedience. Saul put David in charge of a thousand soldiers and sent him to fight the Philistines. No matter how dangerous the battles were, David always won, because God was with him. This made Saul even more afraid of David, but everyone else loved him.

During this time, David became good friends with Saul's son Jonathan. David and Jonathan were like brothers, and they

both loved each other more than themselves. Jonathan even gave David his princely clothes, his armor, and his weapons. One day, Saul ordered Jonathan and his soldiers to kill David, but Jonathan warned David and promised to talk to Saul and change his mind.

The next day, Jonathan reminded Saul of all the good things David had done, including killing Goliath. "Why do you want to kill someone who has done so much to help you and has never hurt you?" Jonathan asked. "God uses David to do great things for Israel!"

"You're right," Saul said. "I promise not to try to kill David anymore." When Jonathan told David about Saul's promise, David returned to his position in the army.

But Saul's promise didn't last. Not long after, David was playing music for Saul and the evil spirit came to upset him. He got so angry that he threw a spear at David again. David ran away and went

to find Jonathan. "What did I do wrong?" David asked. "Why does your father keep trying to kill me?"

Jonathan had a plan. He said, "Tomorrow is a special festival, and everyone will be there. If you don't come, my father will notice and I will be able to see how he feels about you. The next day, if you still aren't there, he will definitely say something, and I will know if it is safe for you to come back. Come hide behind a rock in this field. I will bring a boy with me and shoot some arrows. If I tell the boy, 'The arrows are on this side of you; come back and get them,' then you will know it is safe to return. But if I say, 'The arrows are further away; hurry up and go get them,' you will know that my father still wants to kill you."

The next day at the festival, Saul noticed that David wasn't there, but he didn't say anything about it. The second day of the festival, when David still wasn't there, Saul asked Jonathan, "Where is David? He didn't come to the festival yesterday or today!"

"Please don't be angry," Jonathan said. "David told me he had to go home and asked for permission to miss the festival."

Saul's face turned red with anger, and he exploded at Jonathan. "You are a traitor! I'm ashamed to call you my son! You chose Jesse's son over your own father! Don't you know that your position will never be safe while he's still alive? You should be ashamed of yourself for helping him! He deserves to die!"

The next morning, Jonathan took a boy with him and went to the field where David was hiding. He shot some arrows a long ways and called out, "The arrows are way past you. Hurry up, and don't stop!" The boy retrieved the arrows, but he didn't know about David. When the boy left, David came out of hiding. He bowed down to Jonathan, then the two of them hugged and cried because they knew David would never be safe in the palace again. He had to run away.

David lived on the run for a long time, and Saul kept hunting for him. Sometimes Saul would go out searching with his armies, and other times he stayed home. While David was on the run, many brave soldiers came to live with him, to help him with supplies and protection.

One day, David and his men were camped in a cave. Saul and his army were out looking for David, and they stopped near the cave so Saul could relieve himself. David saw Saul enter the cave, and his men said, "God has surely given Saul over to you today. He promised to give you victory over your enemies. This must be what He was talking about! Kill Saul and you will be king!"

"You don't know what you're saying," David told them. "Saul is my king, and he was put in place by God. I will not do anything against the Lord's king, and I pray I never have to."

David sneaked over and cut off a piece of Saul's robe, then he crept away. When Saul left the cave and started walking down the road, David came out and said, "Your Majesty!" Saul turned and saw him, and David bowed down. "Why do you think I want to harm you, Your Majesty?" David asked. "You can see for yourself that it's not true. While you were

in the cave I cut off this piece of your robe. I could have killed you, but I will not harm God's chosen king. God knows if I've done anything to deserve what you are doing, and I pray that He judges between us and punishes you for trying to kill me. But I won't hurt you."

Saul was ashamed of himself when he heard David's words. He said, "David, you are a better person than I am. If you really were my enemy, you would not have spared my life today. You've always shown me kindness, even when I was cruel to you. I pray that God blesses you for what you've done today."

Saul and his army went home, and he stopped hunting David. David didn't return right away, though. He lived in the land of the Philistines for a while, until he could be sure it was safe to go back to Israel. David was patient. He knew that God would do what He had promised at the right time, so he didn't take matters into his own hands.

DAVID BECOMES KING
1 SAMUEL 30:1-20; 31:1-7; 2 SAMUEL 5:1-10; 1 CHRONICLES 14

David and his men and their families were all living in a town called Ziklag. David came back from traveling to meet with the Philistine kings and found the whole town burned down. He and his men hurried off to find out who had done this, and they found a group of Amalekites celebrating their easy victory. David's men defeated the Amalekites and rescued their families and livestock who had been captured by the Amalekites when they raided the city.

At the same time, Saul and his army were fighting the Philistines. The Philistines were winning. Saul was seriously wounded and feared what they might do to him. He turned to a nearby soldier and said, "Kill me with your sword before the Philistines get up here!"

"I'm sorry, Your Majesty," the soldier replied. "I would do anything for you, but I can't do that."

Saul took his own sword and stabbed himself by falling on it, since the soldier wouldn't kill him and he was afraid to be captured by the Philistines. When the soldier saw what Saul had done, he did the same thing. The Philistines defeated the Israelite army that day, and Saul and three of his sons died in the battle, including David's friend Jonathan.

David heard about what had happened to Saul and Jonathan and how the Israelites had been defeated, so he returned to Israel, to a town named Hebron. The leaders of the family clans of Israel met with David there and said, "You are our brother, and we are your family. While Saul was alive, God promised that you would be our king one day and rule over us. Now please be our king." David and the leaders of Israel agreed, and they poured oil on his head to show that he was now God's chosen king.

At first, David was only the king of Judah, but after seven and a half years, the rest of Israel made him their king, too. David was thirty years old when he first became king. The promise that God had given him through Samuel all those years ago had finally come true. He was patient and waited on God's timing, and God did what He had promised.

There was a group of Canaanites called the Jebusites living in the city of Jerusalem. They had lived there ever since the days of Joshua because they tricked the Israelites into making a treaty with them. David and his army drove the Jebusites out and captured the city. When he had secured Jerusalem, he named it "David's City" and rebuilt it so it could be his capital city. He also fought against the Philistines and defeated them.

God gave David success in everything he did, and David obeyed God. Through his example, he led Israel to obey God, too, just like a good king was supposed to do. David grew more and more famous, and the nations around Israel began to respect and fear him. He was the best king Israel ever had, and it was because he loved God and obeyed Him.

THE BEST AND WORST MOMENTS OF DAVID'S REIGN

1 CHRONICLES 15:1-16:6; 2 SAMUEL 11:1-12:15

When David had built up Jerusalem, he brought the Ark of the Covenant to the city. He set up the tent of worship and prepared priests and people from the tribe of Levi to take care of it. He brought the ark into Jerusalem with a huge parade. People played music and sang as the Levites carried the ark. David danced in front of the ark because he was so happy and wanted to praise God. His wife Michal, the daughter of Saul, was angry. "You're making a fool of yourself," she said. "You should be ashamed to dance in the streets like a commoner."

"I will become even more undignified than this to worship God," David answered. "I don't care what others think of me, as long as God approves!"

David had the Levites and priests put the ark in the tent so everyone could come and worship God there. David loved God so much that he wanted the symbol of God's relationship with His people to be as close to him as possible, and God honored David's love and obedience by blessing him.

No one is perfect, so even though David loved God and obeyed Him, he still made mistakes. One day, David was up on his roof, looking out over the city. He saw a beautiful woman bathing in her courtyard. He asked his servants who she was, and one replied, "That's Bathsheba, Uriah the Hittite's wife." Uriah was one of David's mighty men, the warriors who had joined him while he was running from Saul. David sent for Bathsheba and brought her to the palace. Then he slept with her, even though she was married to Uriah.

A little while later, Bathsheba told David, "I'm pregnant." David knew the baby was his, because Uriah was with the army, fighting at a city called Rabbah. He sent a message to Joab, his general, and said, "Send Uriah to me."

When Uriah arrived, David asked him how the army was, then sent him home. David hoped Uriah would sleep with Bathsheba, and everyone would think the baby was Uriah's. Instead, Uriah slept at the palace. When David asked him why, he said, "Your Majesty, the army is camped in tents, fighting against Rabbah. It wouldn't be right for me to go home and sleep with my wife while my brothers are risking their lives."

David sent Uriah back to Joab with a letter that said, "Put Uriah at the front of the battle, where the defenders are strongest. Then have everyone pull back so Uriah will be killed."

Joab did what David told him, and Uriah died. When David heard the news, he brought Bathsheba to the palace and married her after she had finished mourning for her husband. David killed Uriah to cover up his sin of sleeping with Bathsheba, making his sin even worse.

God sent the prophet Nathan to show David how bad his sin was. "There were two men," Nathan said, "a rich man and a poor man. The rich man had plenty of sheep, but the poor man had only one little lamb that lived in his house with him. The poor man loved his lamb like a child and fed it from his hand. One day, a guest visited the rich man. Rather than cook one of his own sheep, the rich man stole the poor man's lamb and killed it to serve his guest."

David was furious! He said, "Whoever did this deserves to die! Who is it?"

"You are the rich man," Nathan said. "This is what God says, 'I made you king over all of Israel. I protected you from Saul. Why would you disobey me and do something so terrible? You murdered Uriah to steal his wife after you slept with her, even though you knew it was wrong! Because you have done this, your family will never know peace.'"

"I have sinned against God!" David cried.

"Yes, you have," Nathan answered. "He has forgiven you, but the child that is born to you and Bathsheba will die."

David had done something terrible, but instead of trying to hide or do things his own way, he confessed his sin and asked God for forgiveness. God did forgive him, but sin still has consequences. Everything that God told David through Nathan came true.

SOLOMON, THE WISEST KING EVER

1 KINGS 2:10-3:28; 5-6; 10:1-10; 11:1-13

After David died, his son Solomon became the next king. One night God spoke to Solomon in a dream. God said, "Solomon, ask me for anything you want, and I will give it to you."

Solomon said, "Your servant David obeyed you, and you always took care of him. Now I am king in my father's place, and I am your servant, too. I am still very young, and I don't know how to be a leader, but I am in charge of all your people. Please give me wisdom to know right from wrong so I can lead these people in obedience to you."

God was pleased with Solomon's request, and said, "You could have asked for a long life, or riches, or victory over your enemies, but instead you asked for wisdom to lead my people. Because of this, you will be wiser than any person who has ever lived or ever will live. I will also give you the things you didn't ask for: victory over your enemies, a long life, great riches, power, and respect. If you obey me like David did, you will be the greatest king who ever lived."

God was true to His word. He made Solomon so wise that people from all over came to hear his wisdom. All the judges in Israel came to him if they had a decision that was too hard, and Solomon told them how to solve it.

In one of these cases, two women both claimed to be the mother of the same baby. The women lived together, and they both

had babies around the same time. One night, one of the women accidentally rolled onto her baby, suffocating him. The next morning, the mother of the dead baby saw what had happened and switched her dead baby with the living baby. When the other woman woke up, she saw that the dead baby was not her son, but the mother of the dead baby insisted that it was, and that her son was the living baby. No one could figure out who the real mother was, so they brought the women to Solomon. When he had heard the story, Solomon

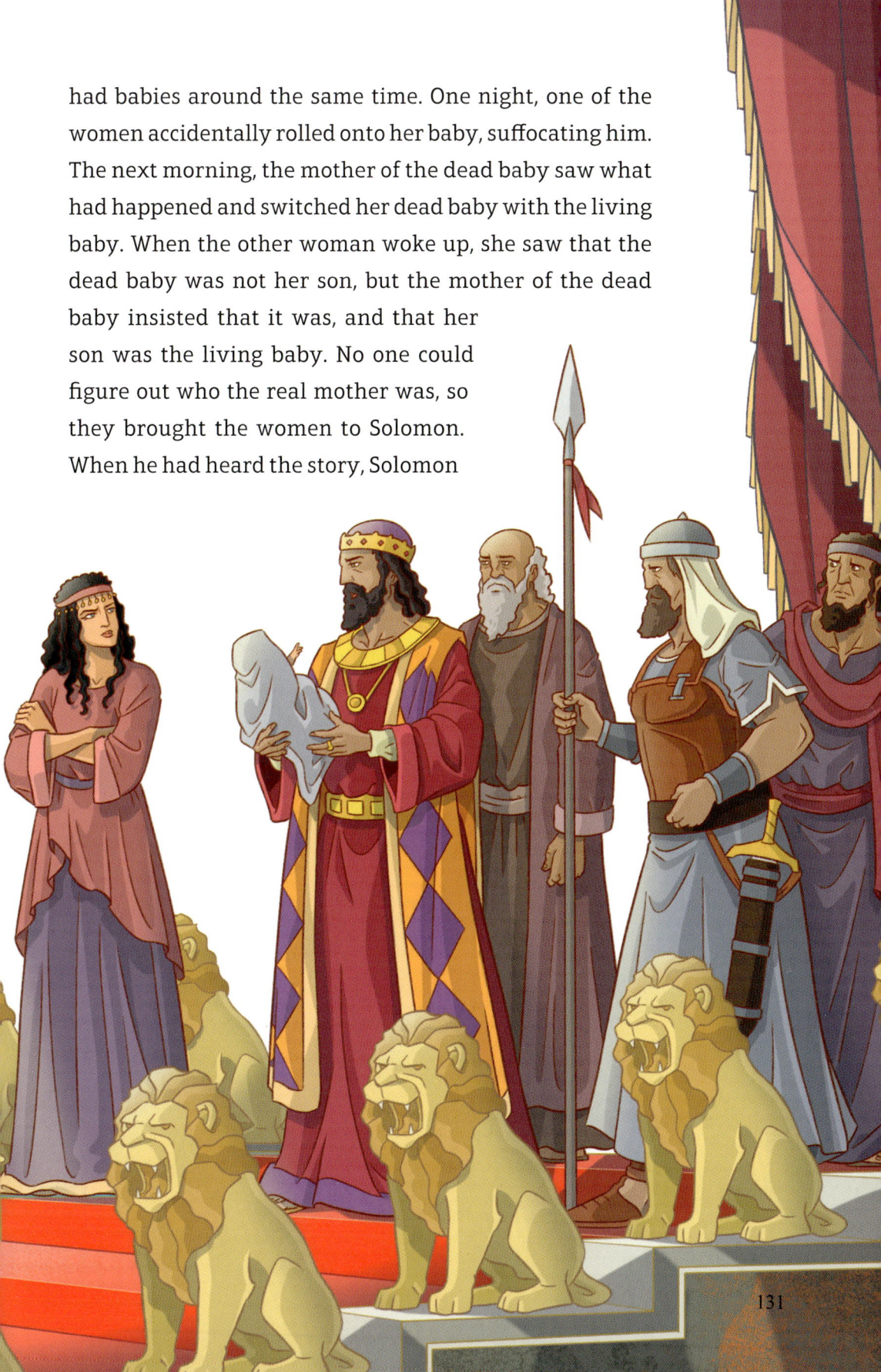

said, "Bring me a sword. Cut the baby in half and give one half to each woman."

The woman whose baby had died said, "Fine, do it."

The woman who was the real mother spoke up and said, "No! Let her have the baby, just don't hurt him!"

Solomon said, "Don't hurt the baby. The woman who would rather give him up than let him be killed is the real mother; give him to her."

While David was alive, he had asked his friend Hiram, the king of Tyre, for supplies to build a temple for God in Jerusalem. Now that Solomon was king, he decided it was time to build that temple. Solomon and Hiram worked together to get all the supplies, and Solomon had all the masons and carpenters he could find working on the temple. When it was done, it was the most beautiful building anyone had ever seen. Solomon celebrated by offering sacrifices and leading the people in prayer. God's glory came down from heaven and filled the temple. God told Solomon, "If you will obey me, following all the commands that I give you, like your father David did, then I will be with you like I was with David. I will live among my people in this temple you have built for me. I will never leave them or abandon them. I will be their God, and they will be my people. We will live together. I will love you, and you will love me and obey me."

Solomon obeyed God and led Israel in obedience to Him, and God blessed them. The temple and Solomon's palace were beautiful works of art, and the city of Jerusalem was the richest city around. Solomon was known far and wide for his great wealth and wisdom, and kings and queens from distant countries visited Israel to see the great king they had heard so much about, to hear his wisdom, and to make treaties with him.

One of Solomon's visitors was the Queen of Sheba. She spent a long time talking with Solomon and asking him questions. After she had seen all the wonders of Solomon's kingdom and had heard his wisdom, she said, "I heard of the greatness of Solomon in my own country, but I didn't

believe it until I saw it with my own eyes! There is so much here that I didn't even know about. You are even wiser and richer than I thought! God has blessed you abundantly!"

As Solomon got older, however, he married more and more foreign wives to make treaties with their nations, and every wife wanted to bring her idols with her from her homeland. Solomon let his wives worship their idols, and soon the rest of the people began to worship idols, too. Even though Solomon was wise, he still made some big mistakes. Because the people of Israel went astray and worshiped idols, God decided that Solomon's son would not rule the whole country. Instead, ten of the twelve tribes rebelled and set up their own king, leaving Solomon's son to rule over the other two. Solomon started off well, but living with God as His people requires a lifelong commitment. Loving and obeying God is not something that we can only do sometimes. We need to do it every day, no matter what.

ELIJAH STANDS UP TO AHAB
1 KINGS 16:29-18:46

Many years after Israel split into two kingdoms, the northern kingdom had a king named Ahab. Ahab led the Israelites to disobey God more than any other king had. He even made everyone worship the idol Baal instead of God. Almost everyone worshiped Baal instead of God, or tried to worship both God and their idols.

Elijah was a prophet who stayed faithful to God. He told Ahab, "I serve the living God, and in His name, I swear that there will be no rain in the whole land until I say otherwise."

Just like Elijah said, there was a drought in Israel for three years. It was so bad that there was almost no food anywhere. When God sent Elijah back to Ahab, Ahab said, "You're the worst troublemaker in Israel!"

"Me?" Elijah said. "You're the real troublemaker. This drought is because you and your family worship Baal. You're leading the nation astray. Call everyone in Israel and have them meet me at Mount Carmel. I have something to show them."

Ahab gathered the people at Mount Carmel. When they got there, Elijah stood up and said, "How long will you try to serve two masters? If the Lord is God, worship Him, but if Baal is God, worship him." No one responded, so Elijah continued, "I am the only prophet of the Lord, but there are 450 prophets of Baal. Let's have a contest. Bring us two bulls. We will each prepare an altar and cut up a bull and put it on the altar with some wood, but we will not light a fire. The prophets of Baal can pray to him, and I will pray to the Lord. The one who responds by sending fire is the real God."

Everyone agreed, and Elijah told the prophets of Baal, "Since there are more of you, you can go first. Pick out your bull and get it ready on your altar. Pray to your god and see if he will light the fire for you."

The prophets of Baal danced around their altar, but nothing happened. They prayed and danced for hours, shouting, "Answer us, Baal!" But their idol didn't answer.

Around noon, Elijah started mocking the prophets of Baal. "Maybe he can't hear you," he said. "You should shout louder! Maybe Baal is using the bathroom or on vacation! I bet he's sleeping. Wake him up!"

The prophets of Baal cut themselves with knives and danced and shouted all afternoon, but Baal still didn't answer. Finally, Elijah said, "It's my turn. Everyone gather around."

Elijah rebuilt an altar to God that had been knocked down. He used twelve stones to represent the twelve tribes of Israel, then he dug a trench around the altar. He cut up his bull and put it on the altar with some wood. Then he had some helpers bring twelve big jars of water and pour water over the altar, the wood, and the offering. When they were done, everything was soaked, and the trench was full of water.

At sunset, Elijah prayed, "Lord, our God, you are the God of Abraham, Isaac, and Jacob. Please show everyone that you are the one true God of Israel. Answer me so your people will see that you are the only real God and turn back to you."

As soon as Elijah finished praying, God sent fire from heaven that burned up the offering, the wood, and the altar. It even dried up the water in the trench. All the people bowed down and said, "The Lord is God!"

"Grab the prophets of Baal!" Elijah ordered. "Don't let them escape."

The people caught all the false prophets who had led them astray and killed them. Then Elijah told Ahab, "You should hurry if you want to get home before the rain comes." Ahab rode home in his chariot. Soon, dark storm clouds rolled in, and rain started pouring all over the whole country. The drought was over.

ELISHA FOLLOWS IN ELIJAH'S FOOTSTEPS

2 KINGS 2; 4:1-7

Elijah began to mentor a young man named Elisha. Elisha followed Elijah everywhere, learning how to be a prophet of God. Elijah knew that he wouldn't be around much longer, so he asked Elisha, "What can I give you before I leave?"

Elisha said, "I want God's Spirit to give me double the power you have so I can be a good leader."

"That's a big request," Elijah said, "but God told me that you will receive it if you see me as I'm being taken up to heaven."

As Elijah and Elisha were walking along, Elijah took his cloak and struck the water of the Jordan River with it. The water parted and they walked across on dry ground. Suddenly, a flaming chariot pulled by fiery horses appeared, separating Elijah and Elisha. Elisha watched as a whirlwind picked up Elijah and carried him to heaven. Elisha cried out, "My master has been taken away by Israel's cavalry and chariots!"

When the whirlwind was gone, Elisha saw Elijah's cloak on the ground. He picked it up and went back to the Jordan River. "I wonder if God will do wonders for me like He did for Elijah," Elisha thought, and he struck the water with Elijah's cloak. The water parted again, and Elisha was able to cross on dry land.

When the other people heard about what had happened, they wanted to look for Elijah, but Elisha knew that God had taken him away. They searched and searched, but Elijah was nowhere

to be found. Elisha became the leader of the prophets of God, and God gave him twice as much power through His Spirit as He had given Elijah.

One day, a woman told Elisha, "My husband followed you and worshiped God, but he owed a man some money. Now he is dead, and his creditor is coming to take away my sons to pay his debt. What can I do?"

"Maybe I can help," Elisha said. "What do you have in your house?"

"Just a small jar of olive oil," the widow answered.

"Ask all your neighbors for empty jars and borrow as many as you can," Elisha said. "Have your sons help you fill the empty jars from your small jar of oil and set aside each jar as you fill it."

The widow and her sons did what Elisha told them, and the oil in their small jar kept flowing until all the borrowed jars were full, then it ran out. The widow sold the oil and made enough money to pay off the debt. She even had some left to live on. God did many other miracles through Elisha because he listened to God and obeyed Him, leading other people to obey God and love Him, too.

JONAH, THE RUNAWAY PROPHET
THE BOOK OF JONAH

One day, God told the prophet Jonah, "Go to the great city of Nineveh and tell them, 'God has seen your sins. You will be destroyed!'" Jonah hated Ninevites, so he didn't want to preach God's message to them. Instead, he found a ship going as far away from Nineveh as possible. The sailors set out for Tarshish, a city in Spain, and Jonah fell asleep below deck.

God sent a huge storm that threatened to break the ship apart. The sailors were terrified. They prayed to their idols and threw cargo overboard to lighten the load. The captain saw Jonah sleeping, so he woke him up and said, "How can you sleep right now? Get up and pray to your God! Maybe He will take pity on us and save us from this storm."

The sailors asked their gods who caused the storm by casting lots. The lot fell on Jonah, and

they asked him, "Is this your fault? What
is your business? Where are you from?"

"I am a Hebrew," Jonah said. "I worship
the God of Israel, who made the sea
and the dry land. And I am running
away from Him."

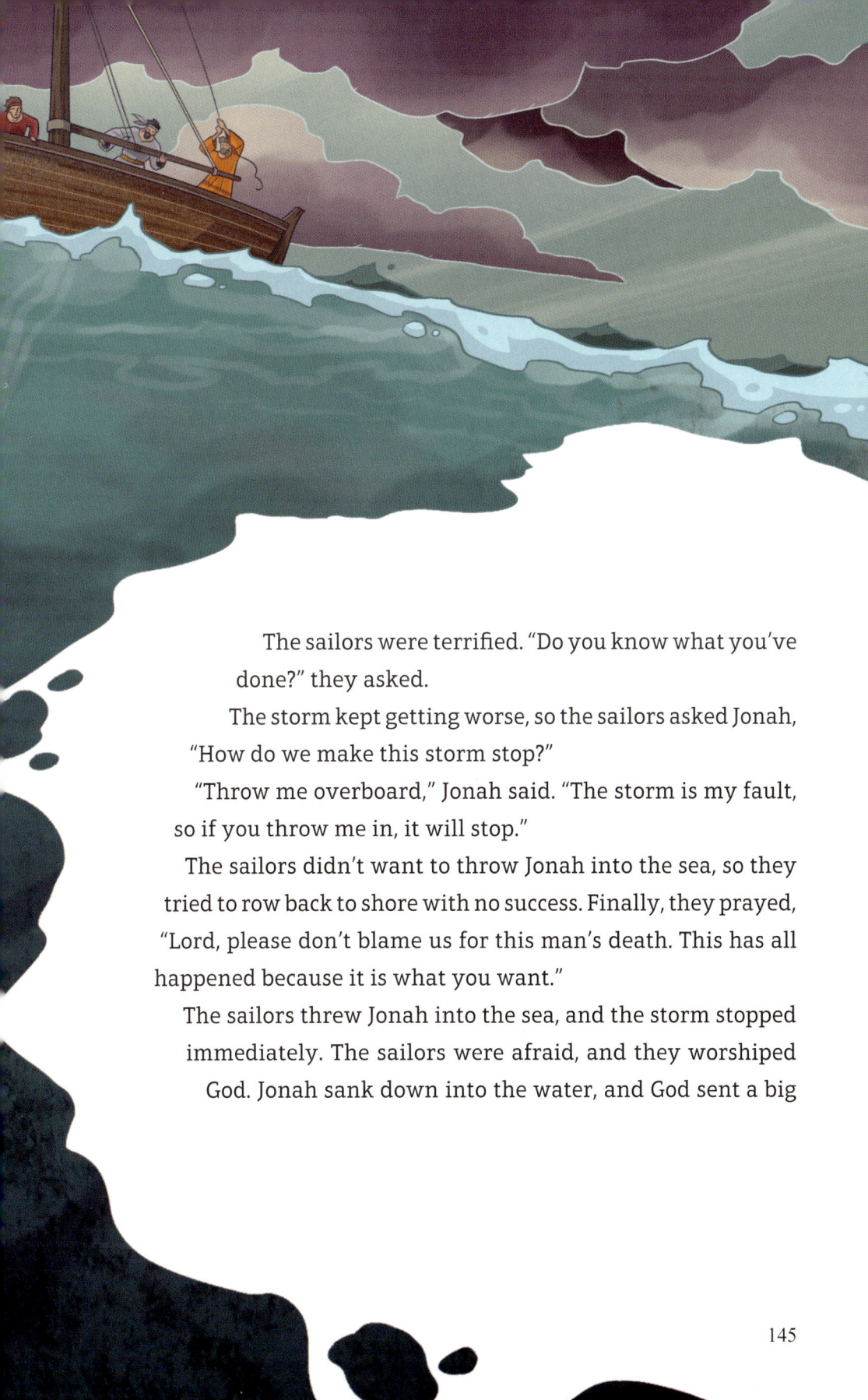

The sailors were terrified. "Do you know what you've done?" they asked.

The storm kept getting worse, so the sailors asked Jonah, "How do we make this storm stop?"

"Throw me overboard," Jonah said. "The storm is my fault, so if you throw me in, it will stop."

The sailors didn't want to throw Jonah into the sea, so they tried to row back to shore with no success. Finally, they prayed, "Lord, please don't blame us for this man's death. This has all happened because it is what you want."

The sailors threw Jonah into the sea, and the storm stopped immediately. The sailors were afraid, and they worshiped God. Jonah sank down into the water, and God sent a big fish to swallow him. Jonah was in the fish's belly for three days and three nights, then he prayed to God.

Jonah said, "Lord, when I was in trouble, I prayed to you and you heard me. You threw me down to the bottom of the sea. There were waves all around me, and I thought I would drown. I thought I would never see your holy temple again. Seaweed wrapped around my head, but you rescued me. You saved me from the pit when my life was slipping away. I prayed to you, and you heard my prayer. Everyone who worships idols turns away from God, but I will praise and worship you. You alone have the power to save."

God ordered the fish to spit Jonah out, so it vomited him up onto the shore. Then God spoke to Jonah again: "Go to Nineveh and preach the message that I gave you."

This time, Jonah obeyed God. Nineveh was such a big city that it took three days to walk through it. Jonah walked into the city for a day and said, "Forty more days and Nineveh will be destroyed!"

It wasn't much of a sermon, but the people believed God's message. The king of Nineveh ordered everyone to fast and wear sackcloth to show how sorry they were. They prayed to God for mercy and stopped being evil and cruel. God saw how the people of Nineveh repented, and He had mercy on them and didn't destroy them after all.

Jonah got angry. "This is why I ran away!" he prayed. "I knew that you are merciful and full of patience and forgiveness. You always show love to people, even these Ninevites. I knew you wouldn't really destroy Nineveh! Just let me die. I would be better off dead!"

"Is it right for you to be angry?" God asked Jonah.

Jonah didn't answer. He left the city and sat on a nearby hill so he could watch what happened to Nineveh. God made a vine grow up to give Jonah shade, and Jonah was happy about the plant. The next day, God sent a worm to chew on the vine, and it withered.

"I wish I was dead!" Jonah said.

"Jonah, is it right for you to be angry about the vine?" God asked.

"Yes!" Jonah answered. "I'm so angry that I could die!"

"You care about this vine that you didn't plant or water or cultivate. It sprang up one day and died the next. There are over a hundred thousand people in Nineveh who don't know right from wrong. Don't you think I should care about them?"

God had compassion on the Ninevites, just like He does on everyone who repents from their sins and turns to follow God. Jonah didn't understand that God loves everyone, even people who are mean. God cares for everyone and is willing to give anyone a second chance if they come to Him.

GOD'S PEOPLE IN EXILE
2 CHRONICLES 36:11-21

The Israelites and their kings kept disobeying God over and over. They worshiped idols and even put idols in God's holy temple, making it unfit for worshiping God. Eventually, God had enough, and He sent the king of Babylon to punish Israel and Judah. All the Israelites from the northern kingdom had been conquered by Assyria, but there were still people in the southern kingdom of Judah, so the king of Babylon came and conquered Jerusalem and Judah. His soldiers destroyed the whole city and the temple and killed a lot of people. The people who were left, they took back to Babylon as captives. The Israelites would live in Babylon for a long time, until Persia conquered Babylon. God used the Persian king Cyrus to send the Israelites back to the Promised Land.

God had warned the Israelites that this would happen several times, from Moses, who warned them when they were about to enter the Promised Land about what would happen if they disobeyed God, to Jeremiah, a prophet who actually lived through the events he warned the people about. God is patient, but He is also holy. His people had been disobeying Him for so long that He had to punish them for their sin. After they had learned their lesson and repented from their sin, He would bring them back. But for now, they were exiles in Babylon.

DANIEL AND HIS FRIENDS SERVE GOD IN BABYLON

DANIEL 1-3; 5-6

When Nebuchadnezzar, the king of Babylon, captured Jerusalem, he took some of the young men back to Babylon. He trained them to work in the royal palace, and ordered that they be given the best food from

his own table. Four of these young men were friends named Daniel, Hananiah, Mishael, and Azariah. The Babylonians gave them new names. They called Daniel Belteshazzar, Hananiah Shadrach, Mishael Meshach, and Azariah Abednego.

Daniel and his friends knew that it was against God's laws for them to eat the king's

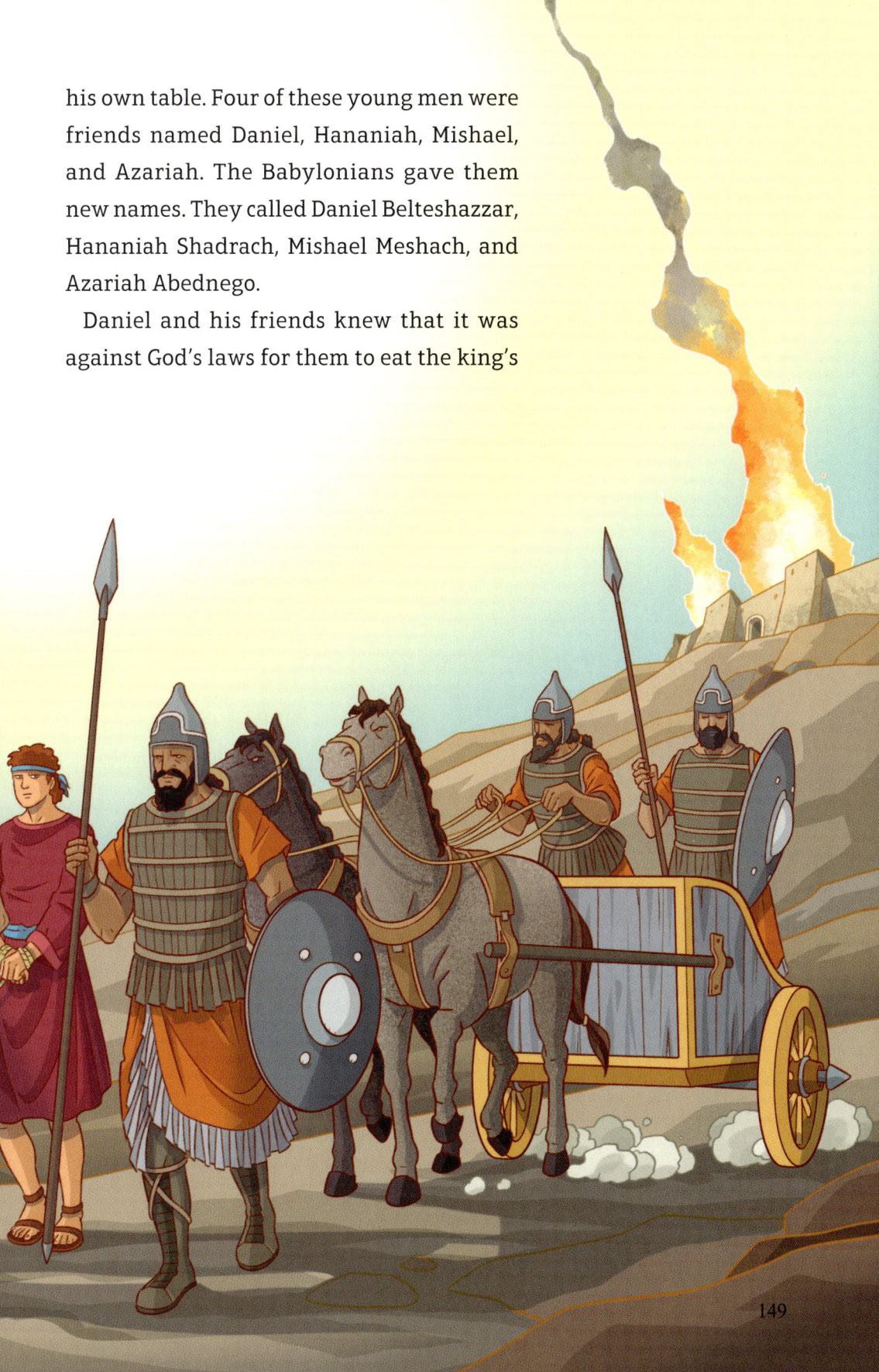

food. Moses had told the Israelites what foods they could eat and what foods were unclean. Some of the king's food was unclean, and some of it had been offered to idols, which was even worse. Daniel and his friends made up their minds that they would not disobey God by eating the king's food, so they asked the official over them for permission to not eat the king's food or drink his wine.

The official said, "Are you trying to get me killed? The king ordered me to give you the best food. If he sees you looking weaker than the others, he'll have me executed."

"Give us ten days," Daniel said. "During that time, we'll only eat vegetables and only drink water. After that, if we don't look as healthy and strong as the other young men, do whatever you think is best."

The official agreed, and for ten days, Daniel and his friends only had water and vegetables. When the time was up, they were healthier and stronger than all the young men who had eaten the king's food. After this they were allowed to eat whatever they wanted.

God blessed Daniel and his friends for their obedience, and they grew smarter and wiser. After three years of training, Nebuchadnezzar interviewed all the young men who had been trained. No one else was as impressive as Daniel, Hananiah, Mishael, and Azariah. Nebuchadnezzar was so pleased that he gave them all positions in his court. Whenever he asked their advice, they were ten times wiser than any of his other advisors.

One night, Nebuchadnezzar had a troubling dream. He called his advisors and magicians together and said, "I had a disturbing dream. Explain what it means."

"Your Majesty, we hope you live forever," the advisors answered. "We are your servants. Tell us your dream, and we will interpret it."

"No," Nebuchadnezzar said. "If you can't tell me what the dream was, as well as what it means, then I will cut you into pieces and tear down your houses. But if you can tell me what my dream was and what it means, I will reward you greatly!"

"Your Majesty," the advisors and magicians replied, "tell us the dream and we can interpret it for you."

Nebuchadnezzar said, "You're trying to trick me into changing my mind. Tell me what I dreamed. Then I will know that you can actually interpret it and not make something up."

"It's impossible, Your Majesty!" they answered. "No king has ever asked his advisors, to do such a thing. It can't be done! Only a god could tell you what you dreamed."

Nebuchadnezzar said, "That's it! All of you are lying and trying to trick me!" He told his guards to round up all the advisors so he could kill them, including Daniel and his friends.

When the guards told Daniel what Nebuchadnezzar had ordered, he said, "Wait, don't kill everyone! I'll tell the king what he dreamed and what it means." Daniel and his friends asked God to show Daniel what the king had dreamed so they would not be executed. That night, God revealed Nebuchadnezzar's dream and its meaning to Daniel.

Daniel returned to the guards and said, "I'm ready to tell the king what he dreamed and give him the interpretation."

The guards brought Daniel to Nebuchadnezzar, and the king said, "Can you truly tell me what I dreamed and give me the interpretation of it?"

"Your Majesty," Daniel replied, "not even the smartest person in the world could do what

you're asking. But God can explain anything. While you were sleeping, He showed you the future. He has shown me the same thing so I can explain it to you.

"In your dream, you saw a huge statue. Its head was gold, and its chest and arms were silver. Its thighs were bronze, and the rest of its legs were iron. Its feet were iron and clay mixed together. While you were watching, a stone appeared that was cut out of a mountain—but not by human hands. This stone hit the feet of the statue and toppled it by crushing the iron mixed with clay. Then it crushed and destroyed the iron, the bronze, the silver, and the gold. The statue blew away like dust, and there was nothing left. Then the stone grew into a huge mountain that filled the whole world.

"That is your dream, Your Majesty, and now I will tell you what it means. You are the greatest king of all time; God has honored you and given you power. You are the head of gold. After you, another kingdom will rise up that is not as strong as yours. Then there will be a kingdom of bronze that rules the whole world. Next there will be a kingdom of iron, but this kingdom will become divided, that's why the statue's feet were clay mixed with iron. At that time, God will set up His own kingdom that will never end. Your Majesty, in your dream, God has shown you what will happen. This interpretation is trustworthy because it was given to me by God Himself."

"Now I know that your God is above all other gods," Nebuchadnezzar said, "because He has given you the power to explain my dream." Nebuchadnezzar was so pleased that he showered Daniel with gifts and honors, making him the governor of the whole province of Babylon and putting him in charge of the wise men.

Nebuchadnezzar became so proud after Daniel explained his dream that he built a huge golden statue of himself that was ninety feet tall and nine feet wide. When it was finished, he told everyone in the city that whenever they heard music they must bow down and worship the golden statue. Anyone who refused to worship the statue would be thrown into a blazing furnace.

Daniel's friends, Hananiah, Mishael, and Azariah, refused to bow down and worship the king's statue. Some of the Babylonian advisors used this as a chance to try to get rid of them. They brought them before Nebuchadnezzar and said, "These Jews are refusing to bow down and worship your golden image."

Nebuchadnezzar was furious. He said, "I will give you one more chance to bow down to my statue. If you don't, I'll throw you into the fiery furnace."

"We don't need a second chance, Your Majesty," the friends answered. "We don't need to defend ourselves. The God we serve is able to save us from the fiery furnace. But even if He doesn't, we still won't worship your gods or bow down to your idols."

Nebuchadnezzar had his guards heat up the furnace seven times hotter than normal and throw the three friends in. The fire was so hot that one of the guards got burned to death just bringing them to the furnace. As soon as they were thrown in and the door was closed, Nebuchadnezzar said, "Wait! Weren't there only three men that we threw in there? Why do I see four men walking around in the furnace? The fourth one looks like a god!"

Nebuchadnezzar got closer and called out, "You three, servants of the Most High God, come out of there!" Hananiah, Mishael, and Azariah walked out of the fiery furnace. Their hair wasn't scorched, and they didn't even smell like smoke. "Praise the God of Israel for sending His angel to protect His servants!" Nebuchadnezzar said. "They would rather die than betray their God. From now on, I will not let anyone say anything against the God of Israel."

Nebuchadnezzar's son Belshazzar became the king after him. Belshazzar liked to throw grand banquets for his officials, and one night he had them bring the golden cups from God's temple in Jerusalem so they could drink wine from them. While they were drinking, they praised their gods that were nothing more than idols.

All of a sudden, a hand appeared and started writing on the wall. Belshazzar was so scared that he grew pale and called for his wise men to tell him what the words meant. "Whoever tells me what this writing means will be given royal robes and a gold chain, and I will make him the third highest person in the kingdom," the king said.

All of the wise men came and tried to figure out what the writing said, but none of them succeeded. Then the king's mother said, "Send for Daniel. He is wiser than anyone else. If anyone can tell you what the writing means, he can."

The king sent for Daniel and offered him a reward for explaining what the writing meant. Daniel said, "You can keep your reward, Your Majesty. You saw the great works that God did to humble your father, and

yet you still thought it would be a good idea to take His holy things and use them for your sinful feast. You didn't even acknowledge the God who gives you breath, so He has sent you this message that you see written on the wall. The message is 'Mene Mene Tekel Uparsin,' and it means, God has numbered the days of your kingdom. He has weighed you on the scales, and you fall short of what it takes to be a true king. God has taken your kingdom away from you and given it to the Medes and the Persians."

That very night, the army of the Medes and the Persians invaded Babylon and killed Belshazzar. Darius the Mede became the new king of Babylon, and Daniel served him as an advisor. Darius made Daniel one of the three highest advisors in the kingdom, and the other

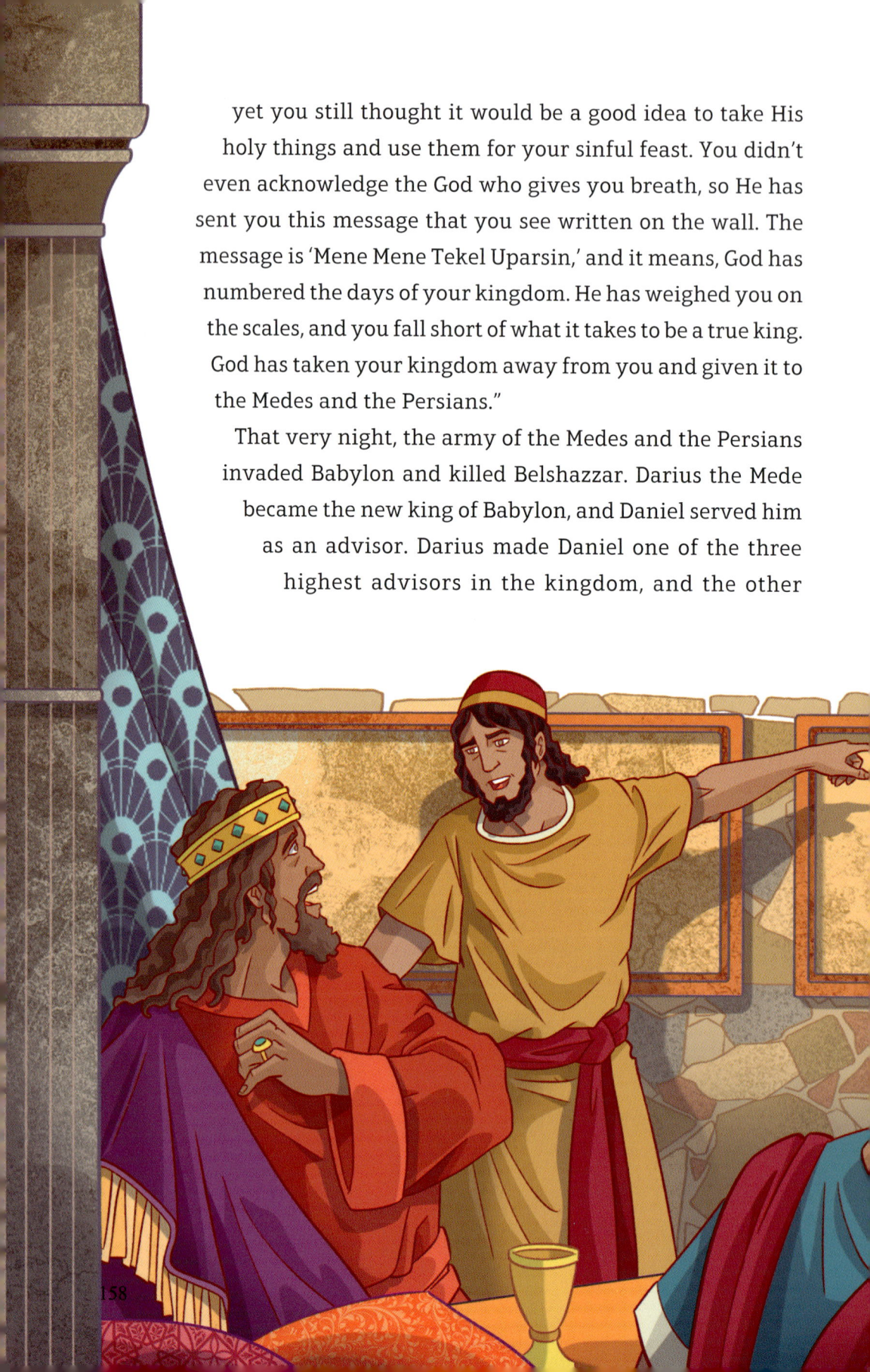

advisors were jealous of Daniel. They were always looking for some way they could accuse Daniel of wrongdoing so they could take his position, but Daniel was honest and faithful in everything he did. Finally, they said to each other, "We will never catch Daniel doing anything wrong unless we make it illegal for him to practice his religion."

The advisors went to Darius and said, "Your Majesty, we have an idea for a new law. For one month, you should make it illegal to pray to anyone, human or god, besides you. If anyone does, they will be thrown in the pit of hungry lions." Darius thought their idea sounded good, so he made it a law.

Daniel heard about this new law, but he still went to his window three times a day and prayed to God, just as he had done since he was a young man. The jealous advisors saw him doing this and told king Darius. Darius liked Daniel, but the law was the law, so he had to throw

him into the lions' den. "Daniel," he said, "you have been faithful to your God, and I pray that He will save you from the lions."

The guards rolled a stone over the mouth of the pit, trapping Daniel inside with the lions. Darius couldn't sleep that night. As soon as the sun rose, he rushed out to the pit and shouted, "Daniel! Was the God you faithfully serve able to save you from the lions?"

"Your Majesty," Daniel called out, "I hope you live forever! My God knew that I was innocent and that I have never done anything to hurt you. He sent His angel to stop the lions from eating me."

Darius was so relieved that Daniel was safe! He ordered his men to get Daniel out of the den right away. Then he ordered the guards to throw the wicked advisors into the lions' den instead. Before they even hit the floor of the pit, the lions had torn them to pieces and devoured them.

Daniel and his friends served God faithfully all their lives. Because they loved Him and obeyed Him, He was with them, even in the land of Babylon. Daniel lived until the first year of king Cyrus of Persia, the king who let the Israelites return to the Promised Land. When we trust God and love and serve Him, He lives with us and takes care of us.

ESTHER AND MORDECAI SAVE GOD'S PEOPLE
THE BOOK OF ESTHER

Xerxes, the king of Persia, ruled from the capital city of Susa. One day, he hosted an enormous banquet and invited anyone who could come. This feast lasted a whole week, and he encouraged everyone to drink as much wine as they wanted. On the seventh day of the party, Xerxes ordered his wife, Queen Vashti, to join him. He wanted to show her off so everyone could see how beautiful she was and admire her fancy clothes and expensive jewelry. But Queen Vashti refused to come.

Xerxes was so angry that he asked his closest advisors what he should do about Vashti. The advisors said, "Your Majesty, Queen Vashti hasn't just embarrassed you, she has set a bad example for all Persian women. If you don't punish her, all wives will think they can disrespect their husbands like Vashti disrespected you. You should get rid of Vashti and find a queen who will respect you."

Xerxes liked this idea, so he kicked Vashti out of the palace. After he calmed down, Xerxes was ready to look for a new queen. "Your Majesty," his advisors said, "let's search the kingdom for beautiful young women and bring them to the palace. You can meet them all, and the one who pleases you the most will be the new queen." So, Xerxes called for all the beautiful young women to come to Susa for a beauty contest to determine who would be his new queen.

When the Israelites returned to their home land, many of them had stayed behind. Esther's parents had stayed in Susa, and when they died,

her cousin Mordecai raised her as his own. Esther was a very beautiful young woman, so she went to the palace for the beauty contest. Esther didn't tell anyone at the palace that she was Jewish. She kept it to herself.

Every young woman at the palace received a year of beauty treatments before she met the king. Then, she got to spend one night alone with Xerxes. When Esther's turn came, Xerxes liked her more than all the other young women, and he fell in love with her right away. Xerxes crowned Esther the new queen of Persia instead of Vashti.

Esther's cousin Mordecai was one of Xerxes' palace officials, and another palace official named Haman had been promoted to the highest position in the kingdom. Haman hated Mordecai. Whenever Haman came through the gate, all of the palace officials were supposed to bow down to him, and they all did except for Mordecai. When the other officials asked him why he wouldn't bow, Mordecai said, "Because I'm a Jew. I will not bow to anyone but God."

Haman was so angry at Mordecai that he wanted to kill all of the Jews in the entire kingdom. He asked Xerxes for permission to write a law ordering the murder of all the Jews in Persia. Xerxes gave him permission, so Haman wrote a law that on a specific day, all the Jews in the whole kingdom would be killed. Haman's decree was shared throughout the whole kingdom, including in Susa. Xerxes didn't give it a second thought, since he didn't realize what it meant for his new queen.

When Mordecai saw Haman's decree, he sent a copy to Esther and told her, "You must plead with the king to have mercy on our people!"

"You don't understand," Esther replied. "Anyone who goes before the king without permission is executed. The only way to save them is for him to hold out his golden scepter to them. The king hasn't sent for me in a month. If I go to him, I could die!"

"Don't think that you will be the only Jew to escape, just because you live in the palace," Mordecai said. "If you stay silent, maybe we will be saved another way. But who knows? Maybe you've been made queen for a time like this!"

"Ask all the Jews in Susa to fast and pray for me for three days," Esther said. "I will also fast and pray with my maidservants. Then I will go see the king, and if I die, I die."

Three days later, Esther went to see Xerxes. The king was happy to see her, and he held out his golden scepter to her. "Esther," he said, "what do you want? I'll give you anything you ask for, even up to half my kingdom!"

"Your Majesty," Esther answered, "please come have dinner with me tonight, and bring Haman with you."

"Go get Haman," the king ordered his servants. "We're having dinner with the queen tonight!"

When Xerxes and Haman were at dinner with Esther, the king asked again, "What can I do for you, Esther?"

"If I have pleased you, Your Majesty," Esther said, "please, will you and Haman come to dinner again tomorrow night? If you do, I will tell you what I really want."

Haman was feeling pretty good about himself when he left Esther's dinner, but his good mood was ruined when he saw Mordecai in the courtyard. When he got home, his wife said, "If you hate Mordecai so much, just ask the king to hang him." So, Haman spent the night building a tall tower by his house so he could hang Mordecai.

Xerxes couldn't sleep, so he had one of his scribes read him the records of the kingdom. The scribe read about a time Mordecai had saved the king's life by telling Esther about a plot to kill him. "Did we ever reward Mordecai for saving me?" Xerxes asked.

"No, Your Majesty," the scribe said.

Just then, Haman came in, intending to ask Xerxes for permission to hang Mordecai. Xerxes said, "Haman, what should I do for someone I want to honor?"

Haman thought Xerxes was talking about him, so he said, "You should dress him in royal robes and let him ride on one of your own horses.

Someone should lead him through the city proclaiming that this is a man you hold in high regard."

"Great idea!" Xerxes said. "Go do all those things for Mordecai."

Haman's plan was ruined. He couldn't ask Xerxes to kill Mordecai now. Instead, he had to lead him around the city and honor him. Haman had a really bad day, but it was about to get worse.

At dinner that night, Xerxes asked Esther, "What can I give you? Whatever you want, even up to half my kingdom, is yours!"

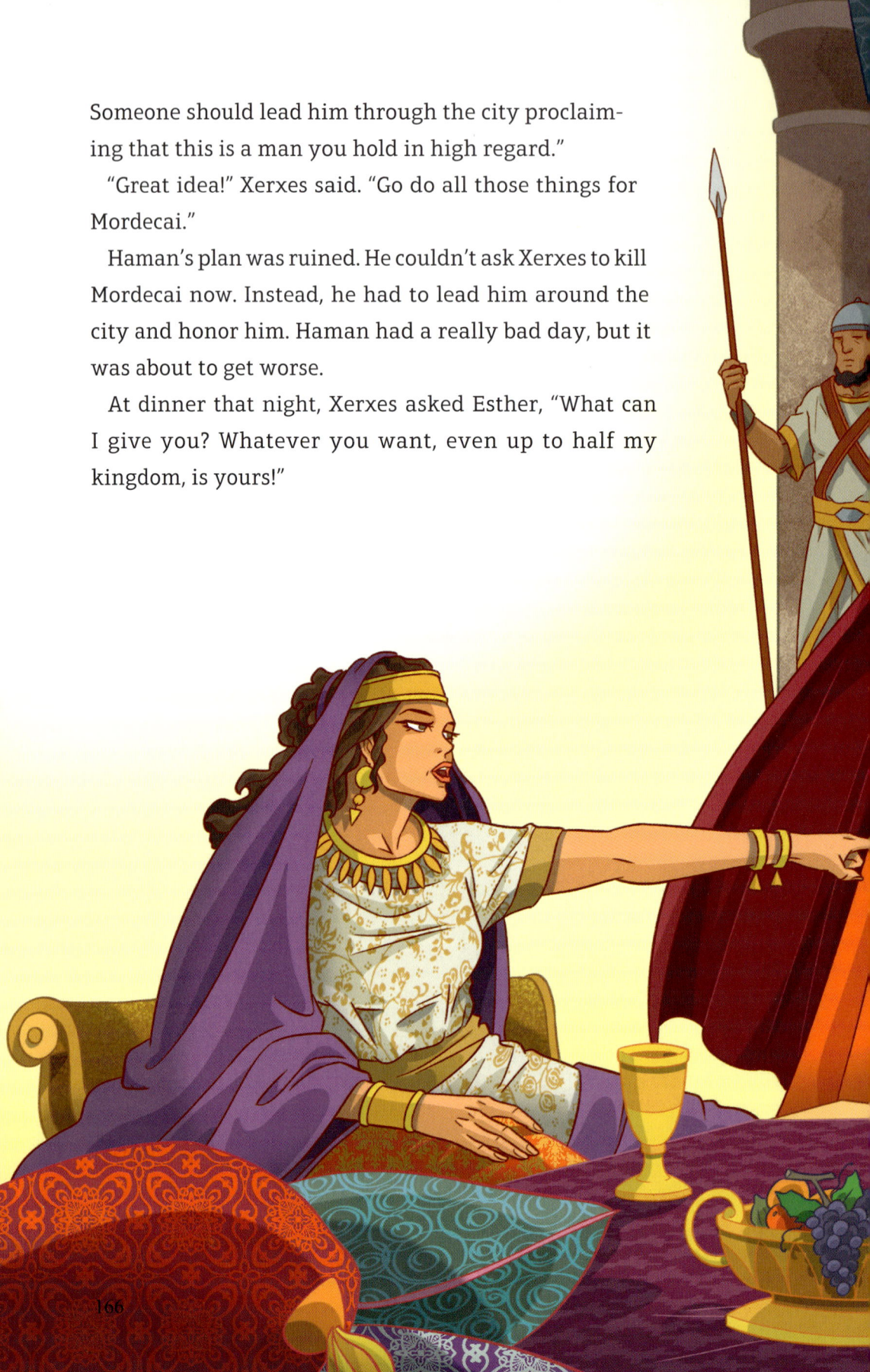

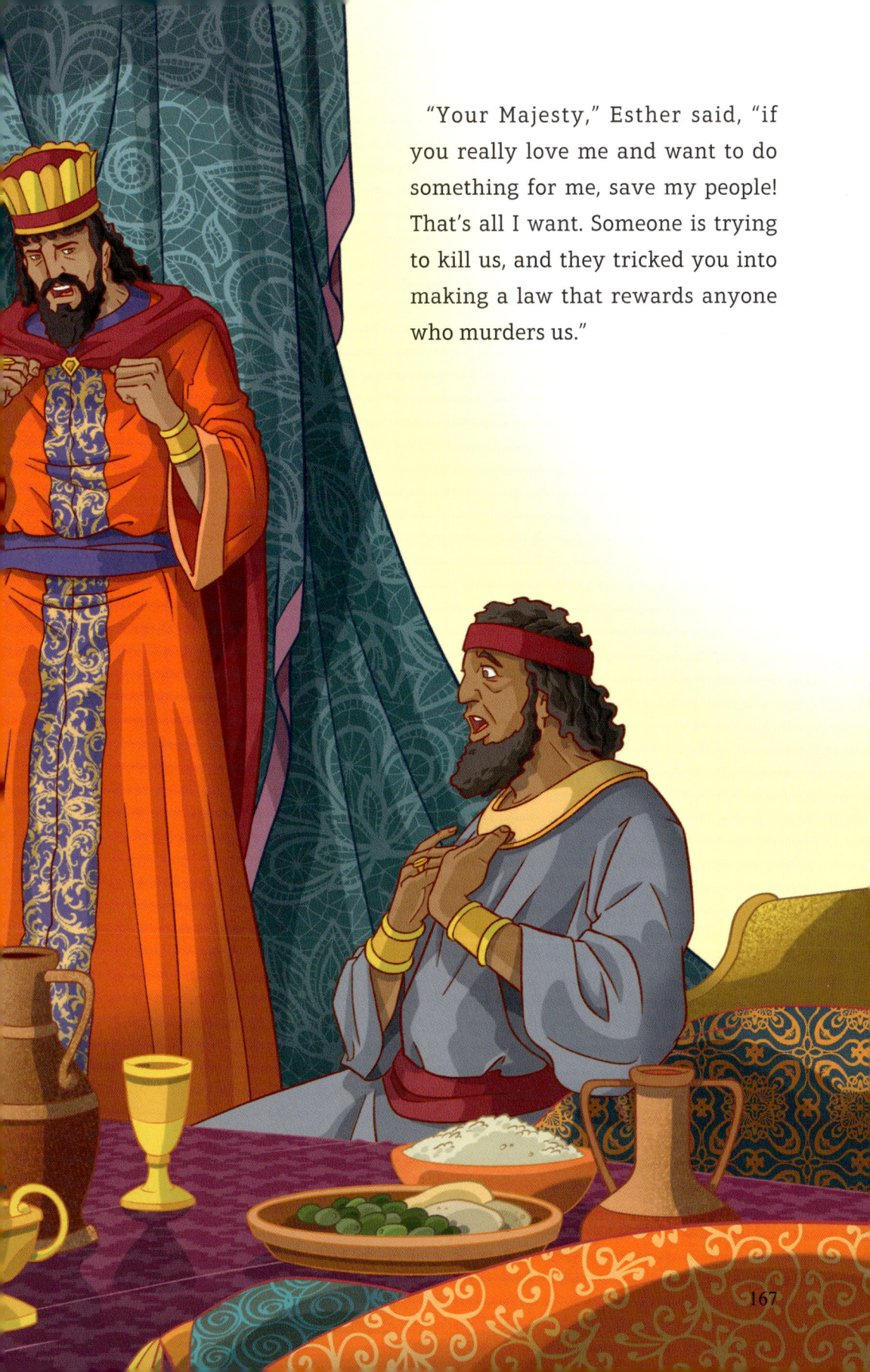

"Your Majesty," Esther said, "if you really love me and want to do something for me, save my people! That's all I want. Someone is trying to kill us, and they tricked you into making a law that rewards anyone who murders us."

167

"Who would dare to do such a terrible thing?" Xerxes asked.

"He would," Esther said, pointing at Haman. "Haman is trying to kill all of the Jews—my people!"

Xerxes was so angry that he got up and walked out onto the balcony for a moment. When he came back in, he saw Haman lunging toward Esther. Xerxes said, "Now you're attacking my queen right in front of me? Take him out of here!"

One of the king's servants said, "Your Majesty, there's a tower next to Haman's house. He wanted to use it to hang Mordecai."

"Take Haman and hang him on his own tower," Xerxes said.

After Haman was executed on the tower he had built for Mordecai, Xerxes asked Mordecai and Esther to help him write a new law to protect the Jews from their enemies. Together, they wrote a law that allowed the Jews to fight back against anyone who tried to hurt them. They sent copies of this law all over the kingdom and the city of Susa. When the day came that Haman's law had specified as the day to kill all the Jews, their enemies attacked them. But the Jews fought back. They defeated

all their enemies in the city and the rest of the country. They no longer had to worry about people trying to kill them.

Esther and Mordecai set up a yearly feast to celebrate and remember the way they had been saved from Haman's scheme. They called this festival Purim. God was still taking care of His people, even all those years after He first made a promise to Abraham, and even all those miles away from the Promised Land. God always loves His people and always wants to save them and have a relationship with them. He used Esther and Mordecai to save them, just like He used many other people in the history of Israel, but He wasn't done yet. Someday, God would provide a way for His people to live with Him in an even better way, a way that would take away their sins and make it so they could have a direct relationship with Him again.

THE NEW TESTAMENT

IMMANUEL: GOD WITH US

LUKE 1:5-45; MATTHEW 1:18-24; LUKE 2:1-20

Centuries after Israel returned from Babylon, they were ruled by the Roman Empire. People were wondering when God would save them like He had in the past. But God had something even better in store: a new way for people to know Him, love Him, and live with Him. It was time for God to send His Son.

In a town called Nazareth, there lived a young woman named Mary. Mary was engaged to a man named Joseph, and she was a virgin. One day, the angel Gabriel appeared to Mary. "Greetings, Mary," Gabriel said. "God is with you!"

Mary didn't know what to say.

"Don't be afraid," Gabriel said. "God is pleased with you, and you will have a son. He will be great, and He will be the Son of God. God will make Him king like His ancestor David, and His kingdom will last forever."

"How is that possible?" Mary asked. "I'm a virgin!"

"God's Holy Spirit will come over you," Gabriel answered, "and His power will create life within you. Your child will be the holy Son of God. Even your relative Elizabeth, who is old, is having a baby; nothing is impossible for God."

Mary trusted God. "I am the Lord's servant," she said. "Let everything happen to me like you said."

Not long after, Mary visited her relative Elizabeth, who was pregnant just like Gabriel had said. As soon as Elizabeth heard Mary's greeting, she cried out, "You are the most blessed of all women, and the child you will bear is blessed! As soon as I heard your voice, the baby inside me leaped for joy! God has blessed you, and I am blessed that the mother of my Lord would visit me!"

When Joseph, Mary's fiancé, heard that she was pregnant, he didn't want to embarrass her publicly. Instead, he decided to break off the engagement quietly. If she had been unfaithful, how could he still marry her? While he was thinking about this, he fell asleep, and an angel appeared in his dream.

"Joseph," the angel said, "do not be afraid to marry Mary. She has not been unfaithful. The child inside her is from the Holy Spirit. Name Him Jesus, because He will save His people from their sins." This all happened to fulfill God's promise through the prophets: "A virgin will be with child and will give birth to a son, and His name will be called Immanuel, which means 'God with us.'" When Joseph woke up, he did what the angel said.

During that time, the Roman emperor ordered the entire empire to return to their home towns to be counted. Because Joseph and Mary were descendants of David, they had to travel south to Bethlehem, the town where David was born. While they were there, the time came for Mary to give birth, but there were no rooms available. One innkeeper let them stay in his stable, so that is where Mary delivered her baby boy. She wrapped Him in cloths and placed Him on a bed of hay in a feed trough.

That same night, there were shepherds watching their flocks in the fields nearby. Suddenly, an angel appeared in the sky above them, and the light of God's glory shone all around them. The shepherds were terrified! But the angel said, "Don't be afraid! I have good news that will give everyone joy! Tonight, in David's City, the Savior has been born! He is Christ, the Lord! You will know who He is because you will find Him wrapped in cloths and lying in a feed trough."

174

Just then, a whole host of angels joined the first one and sang praises to God. When the angels left, the shepherds said, "Let's go to Bethlehem and see this baby God told us about!"

The shepherds found the stable, and Mary and Joseph were there with baby Jesus just like the angel said. The shepherds told Mary and Joseph about the angels, then they returned to their sheep, praising God and telling anyone they met about what they had seen and heard.

God had come down to live with His people. He had sent His only Son, and someday soon, He would take away their sin so they could live with Him again. A new way to know God was here: God was with us.

MATTHEW 2; LUKE 2:40

When Jesus was born in Bethlehem, a bright star appeared in the sky. Far away in the East, a group of wise men saw the star and realized that someone important had been born. They followed the star all the way to Jerusalem, where they asked who the new king was.

Herod was the king in Jerusalem at that time, and he was a selfish, jealous man. When the wise men asked him, "Where is the one who has been born, the king of the Jews? We saw His star in the East and have come to worship Him," he was worried.

Herod asked the chief priests and the experts in the Law of Moses where the scriptures said the Messiah would be born, and they told him, "In Bethlehem, in Judah. The prophet said: 'Oh, Bethlehem, even though you are the smallest city in Judea, you will be the most important. Out of you will come the one who will be a shepherd for my people Israel.'"

Herod told the wise men, "Go to Bethlehem and search for the child, but when you find Him, come back and tell me where He is, because I want to worship Him, too."

The wise men listened to Herod and left Jerusalem. When they did, the star they had seen in the East appeared again, and they were so excited!

They followed the star to Bethlehem until it stopped over the house where Mary, Joseph, and Jesus were living. When the wise men entered the house, they fell down and worshiped Jesus. Then they opened their luggage and gave Him gifts of gold, perfume, and expensive spices.

When the wise men left, an angel warned them in a dream not to return to Herod, so they went back home a different way. Herod was furious that the wise men had tricked him, so he sent men to Bethlehem with orders to kill any baby boys under the age of two years old, since the wise men had told him the star had first appeared about two years ago.

After the wise men left, an angel appeared to Joseph in a dream and warned him that Herod was searching for Jesus and wanted to kill Him. "Go to Egypt," the angel said, "and stay there until I tell you it is safe to return." So, Mary and Joseph and Jesus went to Egypt and stayed there until Herod died. The angel appeared again in a dream and told Joseph it was safe now, so Joseph took his family back to Israel. But, when he found out that Herod's son was the new king, he didn't go back to Bethlehem. Instead, he went back to his hometown of Nazareth and settled down there.

MY FATHER'S HOUSE

LUKE 2:41-52

When Jesus was twelve years old, His parents took him to Jerusalem to celebrate Passover. They traveled with a big group of friends and family, so when they didn't see Jesus on the way back, they thought He was with someone else. When they stopped for the night, however, Jesus was nowhere to be found!

Mary and Joseph hurried back to Jerusalem and searched high and low for Jesus. "Where could He be?" they wondered. Finally, they found Him in the temple, talking to the priests and the teachers of the law. Everyone who was listening to them was amazed at how wise He was and how well He knew the law.

"There you are!" Mary said. "Don't you know your father and I have been looking everywhere for you? We've been worried sick!"

"Why were you looking for me?" Jesus asked. "Didn't you know that I would be in my Father's house?"

Jesus returned home with Mary and Joseph. He continued to grow stronger and wiser, and He gained favor with God and people.

THE LAMB OF GOD

MATTHEW 3:1-17; JOHN 1:19-34

Mary's relative Elizabeth also had a baby boy, and his name was John. When John grew up, God called him to go out into the wilderness near the Jordan river and tell people to turn away from their sinful way of life and get ready for the kingdom of God to come. John wore clothes made from scratchy camel hair, and he ate locusts and wild honey. Many people came out to hear him teach, and when people believed his message, he baptized them in the river to show that they were turning away from sin to follow God.

Some people thought that John might be the promised Messiah, the chosen one of God who would save His people and live with them forever. When they asked John about it, he said, "I am not Him. I am just a voice calling out in the wilderness to prepare the way, like Isaiah the prophet said. Someone else is coming after me, and I am not even worthy to untie His sandals!"

The next day, John saw Jesus walking down to the river, and he said, "Look, there He is! That's the lamb of God who will take away the sins of the world!"

Jesus asked John to baptize Him, and John said, "I shouldn't baptize you! You should be the one baptizing me!"

"This is what God wants us to do," Jesus answered, so John baptized Jesus in the Jordan river.

When Jesus was coming up out of the water, the sky opened up and God's Spirit, looking like a dove, came down and landed on Jesus. A voice from heaven—God's voice—said, "This is my Son, whom I love. I am very pleased with Him!"

God did this to show people who Jesus was and what He had come to do. He was the one God would use to save His people and live with them forever.

SATAN TEMPTS JESUS
LUKE 4:1-15

After Jesus was baptized, God's Spirit led Him into the wilderness for forty days and nights. During that time, He didn't have anything to eat, so by the end He was very hungry. Satan, the tempter, appeared to Jesus. Satan wanted Jesus to sin and break His relationship with God.

Satan said, "You must be starving! Aren't you the Son of God? Just order one of those stones to become bread for you to eat."

Jesus replied, "The Scriptures say that people cannot live on only bread. They need God's word in order to live."

Next, Satan brought Jesus to the top of a tall mountain and showed Him all the kingdoms of the world. "This is all mine," Satan said, "and I'll give it to you if you bow down and worship me."

Jesus answered, "The Scriptures say to love the Lord and serve only Him."

Satan took Jesus to the top of the temple, the highest place in Jerusalem. "If you are God's Son," he said, "jump down from here. After all, the Scriptures say that God will order His angels to watch over you so that you won't even stub your toe on a rock."

Jesus answered, "The Scriptures also say not to test God."

Satan was out of tricks. Jesus had passed all his tests. God's Spirit led Jesus home to Galilee, and He started teaching people the good news about God's kingdom.

FOLLOW ME
JOHN 1:35-51; LUKE 5:1-11

After John told the people listening to him that Jesus was the lamb of God, two of his followers went and found Jesus. "What do you want?" He asked them.

"Where are you staying, teacher?" they asked.

"Come and see," He answered.

The two men stayed with Jesus all day, and when they went home, one of them, a man named Andrew, told his brother Simon, "We have found God's chosen Messiah!"

Not long after this, Jesus was teaching people on the shore of the sea of Galilee, and the crowd was so big that He asked a nearby fisherman to let Him use his boat so He could teach the people without being crowded. That fisherman was Simon. Simon rowed the boat out a little ways and Jesus sat down in the boat to teach the people on shore. When He was done teaching them, Jesus told Simon to go out into the water and put down his nets to catch fish.

"Teacher," Simon answered, "we've already been fishing all night, but we didn't catch anything. But if you say so, we will put down the nets."

As soon as he did, he caught so many fish that the nets were close to breaking. Simon called to his friends in another boat to help him bring the catch of fish back to shore. They filled both boats so full that they were almost sinking from all the fish. When Simon saw this, he was afraid. "Don't come near me, Lord," he told Jesus. "I am a sinner."

"Don't be afraid," Jesus answered him. "Follow me, and from now on, you will catch people instead of fish. Your name is Simon, but from now on, you will be called Peter."

183

Simon Peter, his brother Andrew, and their partners, James and John, the sons of Zebedee, left their boats and nets to follow Jesus. Their lives would never be the same.

The next day, they met a man named Philip. "Follow me," Jesus said, and Philip did.

Philip went and found his friend Nathanael and said, "We've found the Messiah that Moses and the prophets wrote about! He is Jesus, the son of Joseph and Mary from Nazareth."

"Nazareth?" Nathanael asked. "Is there anything good that has ever come from there?"

"Come and see!" Philip answered.

Jesus saw Nathanael coming with Philip, and He said, "Here comes a true Israelite, someone who is completely honest."

"Teacher," Nathanael said, "do you know me?"

"I saw you before Philip called you, when you were sitting under the fig tree," Jesus answered.

Nathanael was shocked. "Teacher!" he said, "you are the Son of God and the King of Israel!"

"Do you believe just because I told you I saw you under the fig tree?" Jesus asked. "I tell you the truth, you will see even greater things than that!"

A WEDDING MIRACLE
JOHN 2:1-11

Jesus and His followers went to a wedding in the nearby town of Cana. While they were there, the wine ran out for the wedding feast. Jesus' mother, Mary, knew that He would be able to help. She told Him, "They ran out of wine!"

"Why are you involving me?" Jesus asked. "It's not time for me to reveal my power yet."

Mary told the servants to do whatever Jesus told them.

Jesus pointed to six big stone jars. "Fill those up with water," He said. When the jars were full, Jesus said, "Bring some of the water to the person in charge of the feast."

The servants brought a cup of the water to the person in charge of the feast. When he tasted it, the water had become wine! The person in charge of the feast didn't know where the new wine had come from, so he went to the groom and said, "Normally people put out the good wine first and save the cheaper stuff until later, but you saved the best for last!"

This was the first miracle Jesus did in public, but only His followers and the servants knew what He had done. When His followers saw it, they believed in Him even more.

JESUS CLEARS THE TEMPLE
JOHN 2:13-22

Jesus went to Jerusalem to celebrate Passover. There He saw people selling animals and exchanging money in the temple. He made a whip out of rope and chased the animals and merchants out of the temple. He knocked the moneychangers' tables over and told the bird sellers to leave.

"My Father's house is a house of prayer!" Jesus said. "Don't make it into a market!"

His followers remembered that the scriptures said, "I am filled with passion for Your house."

The Jewish leaders said, "What right do you have to do these things? Show us a sign."

"Destroy this temple," Jesus said, "and I will build it again in three days."

The people thought He meant the temple building that had taken many years to build. What He was really talking about was His body. He was predicting that He would die and come back to life after three days. Later, His followers would remember this, but for now, no one understood.

LIVING WATER

JOHN 4:4-42

Jesus and His followers were traveling through Samaria. Samaria used to be part of the northern kingdom of Israel, but now the Jews and Samaritans didn't get along. Jews usually refused to have anything to do with Samaritans. Jesus and His followers stopped at a Samaritan village called Sychar. Jesus stayed by the well, and His followers went into town to buy food.

While Jesus was alone, a woman from the town came to get water. Jesus asked her for a drink, and she replied, "Sir, you are a Jew and I am a Samaritan. Why would you ask me for a drink?"

Jesus answered, "If you knew what God wanted to give you, and who had asked you for a drink, you would have asked me for a drink instead, and I would have given you living water."

"Sir," the woman said, "you don't have a bucket, and the well is deep. Where can you get this living water? Our ancestor Jacob dug us this well. Are you greater than him?"

"Everyone who drinks this water will get thirsty again," Jesus said. "Whoever drinks the water that I offer will never get thirsty again. My living water is like a fountain that bubbles up inside of you and gives you eternal life."

"Sir, give me this water!" the woman said. "Then I won't have to keep coming back to this well."

"First bring your husband here," Jesus said.

"I don't have a husband," the woman replied.

"You're right to say you don't have a husband," Jesus told her. "In fact, you have had five husbands, and the man you live with now is not your husband."

"Sir, you are a prophet!" the woman said. "Please tell me something. My ancestors worshiped God on this mountain, but the Jews say that God must only be worshiped in Jerusalem. Who is right?"

"You Samaritans do not really know the one you worship," Jesus said. "We Jews know the God we worship, and through us, He is doing something important. I tell you the truth, there is a time that is coming and is already here, when people will not worship God only on this mountain or in Jerusalem. The Spirit of God will lead His worshipers to worship Him in the Spirit and in truth. God is Spirit, so those who worship Him must worship Him in the Spirit and in truth."

"I know that the Messiah is coming," the woman said, "and when He comes, He will explain everything."

"You are already speaking to Him," Jesus said.

Just then, Jesus' followers returned. The woman filled up her water jar, left it by the well and ran back to town.

"Come quickly!" she told everyone. "Come see a man who told me everything I had ever done! Could He be the Messiah?"

All the people in Sychar came out to see Jesus. While they were coming, Jesus' followers tried to offer Him some food.

"I have food to eat that you do not know about," Jesus told them.

His followers were confused. "Did someone else bring Him food?" they wondered.

"My food is to do what God sent me to do!" Jesus said.

Jesus spoke to the people of Sychar, and many of them believed in Him. He stayed with them for two days, and even more Samaritans put their faith in Jesus. They told the woman who had met Jesus at the well, "We no longer believe just because of what you told us. We have heard Him for ourselves, and we believe that Jesus is the Savior of the world!"

LOWERED THROUGH THE ROOF
LUKE 5:17-26

One time, Jesus was teaching in a house. There were so many people gathered to hear Him that the house was completely full. Four men carried their paralyzed friend on a mat so he could see Jesus. When they saw that they could not get in the door, the men carried their friend up the outside stairs to the roof of the house. They made a hole in the roof and lowered the mat with their friend on it down through it.

When Jesus saw how the man and his friends had faith in Him, He told the paralyzed man, "Your sins are forgiven."

Some of the teachers of the Law wondered to themselves, "How can He forgive someone's sins? Only God can do that."

Jesus knew what they were thinking, so He said, "Is it easier to tell this man his sins are forgiven, or to get up, pick up his mat, and walk?

I will show you that I have the authority to forgive sins." He turned to the paralyzed man and said, "Get up. Pick up your mat and walk."

Right away, the paralyzed man was healed. He got up and picked up his mat. He and his friends walked home together, praising God.

LEVI MEETS JESUS
MARK 2:13-17

Jesus was walking near the sea of Galilee another time, and He saw a man named Levi collecting taxes from people at his booth. "Follow Me," Jesus said, and Levi got up and left his booth to follow Jesus.

Later, Jesus and His followers were having dinner at Levi's house, along with many of Levi's old friends and coworkers. Some of the teachers of the Law asked Jesus' followers, "Why does your master eat with tax collectors and sinners?"

Jesus heard what they were saying and answered, "Healthy people don't need a doctor, but sick people do. I have not come to save righteous people. I have come to save sinners."

PICK UP YOUR MAT
AND WALK

JOHN 5:1-9

Another time, when Jesus was in
Jerusalem, He saw a man lying on a mat
near a pool. The man had been sick for thirty-eight years. Sometimes an
angel would stir up the pool, and the first person who got in would be
healed. The man wanted to get in, but someone else always got in first,
because he was paralyzed.

Jesus asked the man, "Do you want to be healed?"

"I do, Lord," the man said, "but I don't have anyone to help me get in
the pool. Someone always gets
there first."

"Pick up your mat and
walk!" Jesus said.

Right away, the man
was healed.

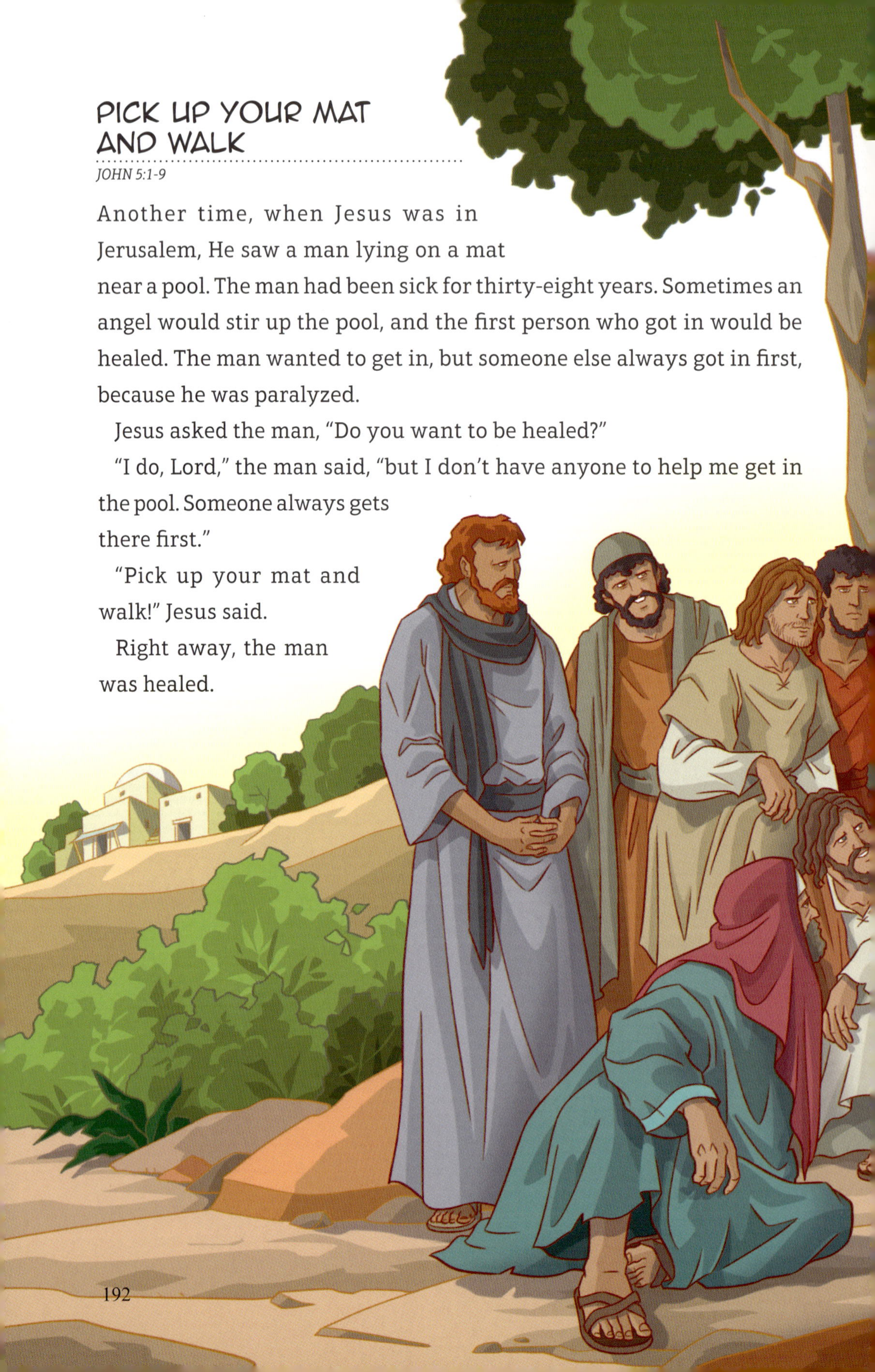

THE DISCIPLES

LUKE 6:12-16; 9:2-6

Jesus went up on a mountain to pray, and He spent the night in prayer. In the morning He called His disciples, and He chose twelve of them. He chose Simon Peter and Andrew, James and John, Philip, Bartholomew, Matthew, Thomas, James son of Alphaeus, Simon the Passionate, Jude, and Judas Iscariot, who would later betray Him.

Jesus sent the disciples out to tell people about God's kingdom, and He gave them power to heal sick people. He told them, "Don't take anything with you—no supplies or food. If someone welcomes you, stay with that person as long as you are in town. If no one welcomes you, move on to the next town."

The twelve disciples did what Jesus said. They preached the good news all over, telling people about God and healing those who were sick.

JESUS TEACHES ON A MOUNTAIN
MATTHEW 4:23–5:16; 6:19-30; 7:24-29

Jesus went all around Galilee, teaching people and healing those who were sick. Huge crowds followed Him around, listening to Him teach about God's kingdom. When Jesus saw the crowd that had gathered, He went up on the side of a mountain in Galilee and sat down to teach them.

Jesus said, "God blesses those who depend on Him. They are part of His kingdom. God blesses those who grieve. He will comfort them. God blesses the humble. He will give them the whole world. God blesses those who are hungry and thirsty to do the will of God. He will give them what they want. God blesses those who are merciful. He will give them

mercy. God blesses those who have pure hearts. They will see Him! God blesses those who are peaceful. They will be called His children. God blesses those who are mistreated for doing what is right. They are part of His kingdom. God will bless you when people mistreat you, mock you, and tell lies about you because you follow me. You will have a reward in heaven! People did those same things to God's prophets long ago.

"You are like salt for the world to taste. But if salt loses its saltiness, it cannot be made salty again. It is only good for throwing on the ground. You are like a light for the world to see. You cannot hide a city on a hill, and no one lights a lamp and hides it under a clay pot. Instead, they put it on a lampstand to light up the whole room. Let your light shine before people like that. When they see the good things you do, they will praise God!

"Don't save up your treasures here on earth. Moths and rust destroy things, and thieves break in and steal them. Instead, save up treasures

in heaven, where moths and rust will not destroy them and thieves will not break in and steal them. Wherever your heart is, that is where your treasure is, too. No one can serve two bosses. They will always like one more than the other and be more faithful to one than the other. You cannot serve both God and money.

"Don't worry about anything. Don't worry about what you will eat or what you will wear. Isn't life about more than just food and clothes? Look at the birds! They don't worry about where their food comes from, but God takes care of them. Aren't you more important than birds? And why worry about clothes? Look at the flowers! They do not work to make clothes, but even King Solomon in all his riches didn't have clothes as beautiful as theirs. If God takes such good care of plants that grow up one day and are gone the next, won't He take care of you, too?

"If you listen to my teaching, you will be like a wise person who builds a house on solid rock. When storms come with strong winds and rain, the house stands strong because it is built on the rock. If you ignore my teaching, you are like a foolish person who builds a house on sand. When storms come with strong winds and rain, the house comes crashing down because it has no foundation."

When Jesus was done teaching the people, they were all amazed. He taught them with authority, not like the teachers of the Law of Moses.

JESUS USES STORIES TO TEACH

LUKE 7:36-50; MARK 4:1-20; MATTHEW 13:24-43

Jesus used stories to teach people about God's kingdom. These stories communicated important lessons about God and how to love Him and live with Him. One day, Jesus was eating with His disciples at a religious leader's house. While they were eating, a woman from the town who had a reputation for being sinful came in. She saw Jesus and knelt down at His feet. She started to weep and washed His feet with her tears. She dried Jesus' feet with her hair then took a bottle of expensive perfume and poured it on His feet and kissed them.

The man who had invited Jesus thought, "If this man really was a prophet, He would know what kind of woman is touching Him and what a terrible sinner she is!"

Jesus knew what His host was thinking. He said, "I have a story for you. Two people owed money to the same moneylender. One owed him five hundred silver coins, and the other owed fifty. Neither one could pay him back, so the moneylender canceled both of their debts. Which one of them will love him more?"

"I suppose the one who had a bigger debt forgiven," the host said.

"You are correct," Jesus said. He turned to the woman and continued, "Have you noticed

this woman? When I came into your house, you did not offer me any water to wash my feet, but she washed my feet with her tears. You did not greet me with a kiss, but she has not stopped kissing my feet since she arrived. You did not give me oil for my head, but she has given me expensive perfume. All her sins are forgiven, and that is why she is showing me so much love. Someone who is only forgiven a little will show only a little love."

Jesus said to the woman, "Your sins are forgiven."

The other guests wondered, "Who is this man who dares to say He can forgive sins?"

Jesus told the woman, "Because of your faith in me, you are now saved. May God's peace be with you."

Another time, when Jesus was in Galilee, He used a story to teach the people. He said, "A farmer went out to sow seeds in his field. Some of the seed fell on the road, and the birds swooped down and ate it. Some of the seed fell on rocky ground, where it grew quickly because of the shallow soil, but it had no roots. When the sun came up, it scorched the plants, and they withered. Some of the seed fell on weedy ground, but

thorn bushes grew up and choked the plants. Finally, some of the seed fell on good soil, and the plants grew and produced a good crop."

Later, when Jesus was alone with His disciples, He told them, "I will tell you the meaning of these stories, but with other people I keep it a secret. After all, the scriptures say that people will 'look but not see and listen but not hear. If they saw and heard, they would turn and believe.' If you do not understand this story, you will not understand the others either. The seed represents the good news about God's kingdom. The seed that falls on the road represents people who hear the good news, but Satan immediately snatches it away, and they do not understand the message. The seed that falls on rocky ground represents people who hear the message, and receive it with joy, but they don't have roots. When life gets hard, or people treat them poorly because of the message, they abandon it. The seed that falls in the thorn bushes represents people who hear the message and receive it right away but are worried about the things of this world. Their worries choke out the message, and they never produce fruit. The seed that falls on the good soil represents people who hear the message and accept it fully. They grow and produce a lot of fruit."

Another time, Jesus told this story: "A farmer sowed wheat seeds in his field, but that night, his enemy came and sowed weeds on top of the good seed. When the wheat started sprouting, so did the weeds. The farmer's workers asked him, 'Do you want us to pull up the weeds?' 'No,' he answered. 'You might accidentally pull up the good plants along with them. Let the weeds and the wheat grow together. Then at harvest time, separate the good grain into bundles and store it in my barns, and separate the weeds into bundles to be burned.'"

Later, the disciples asked Jesus about story of the wheat and the weeds. He told them, "The farmer represents the Son of Man, and the good seeds represent those who belong to God's kingdom. The field is the world,

and the weeds represent those who belong to the evil one. Satan is the one who scattered the weeds. The harvest represents the end of time, when the Son of Man will send out angels to gather all the people who do evil and throw them out of the kingdom. But the people who do what is right belong to the kingdom of God and will live with Him forever. If you have ears, listen!"

Jesus used another story to explain things to them. "God's kingdom is like a mustard seed," He said. "It is the smallest seed, but when the farmer plants it, it grows into a plant as big as a tree! The birds even come and rest in its branches. God's kingdom is also like yeast. A baker mixes just a little yeast into three whole batches of dough, but after a little while, the whole thing rises." Jesus used lots of stories like this to teach people. In fact, He used them every time He taught.

JESUS HAS AUTHORITY

MARK 4:35–5:20

One night, Jesus and His disciples were sailing across the sea of Galilee. During the night, they ran into a huge storm with strong wind and waves that almost sank the boat. The disciples were afraid, so they looked around for Jesus and found Him sleeping in the back of the boat. "Teacher!" they said. "Don't you care if we drown?"

Jesus got up and talked to the storm. He said, "Calm down. Be still." Right away, the storm stopped. "Why were you afraid?" Jesus asked the disciples. "Don't you have any faith?"

When they reached their destination, Jesus and His disciples met a man who was possessed by evil spirits. This man lived in the graveyard, and no one in town could tie him up anymore. He had broken out of everything they tried, even iron shackles! He spent all day and night wandering naked around the graveyard and hills near town, screaming and cutting himself with sharp stones.

As soon as the man saw Jesus, he dropped to his knees and shouted, "Jesus, Son of God, what do you want from me? Promise in God's name that you won't hurt me!" It was actually the evil spirits inside of him who were talking. They knew who Jesus was, and they were afraid, because He had already told them to come out of the man.

"What is your name?" Jesus asked.

"Legion," the man answered, "because there are many of us." The evil spirits begged Jesus not to send them away. There was a

herd of pigs on a nearby hillside, so the evil spirits said, "Please let us go into the pigs instead! Send us into them!"

Jesus let the evil spirits go into the pigs, and the whole herd—two thousand pigs—rushed down into the water and drowned. The men who were watching the pigs ran into town to tell people what had happened. When they got back, they saw the man who had been possessed by evil spirits. He was sitting with Jesus, fully clothed, and in his right mind again. When the people realized what had happened, that Jesus had power over the evil spirits, they were afraid and asked Him to leave their town.

Jesus and His disciples got back in their boat, and the man who had been freed from the evil spirits wanted to come with them. Jesus told him, "Go home to your family and tell them about how good God is and what He did for you." The man did what Jesus said, and everyone who heard what Jesus had done for him was amazed. Jesus has power and authority over everything, even storms and evil spirits, because He is the Son of God.

JESUS HEALS THE BLIND
MATTHEW 9:27-31

Once, when Jesus was walking along, two blind men called out, "Jesus, Son of David, have mercy on us!"

"Do you believe that I can heal you?" Jesus asked them.

"Yes, Lord," they answered.

Jesus touched their eyes and said, "Because of your faith, you are healed." Right away, they could see again! Jesus ordered them not to tell anyone what He had done, but they were so excited that they couldn't help it.

HEROD KILLS JOHN THE BAPTIST

MARK 6:14-29

Jesus was getting so popular that king Herod, the descendant of the king who had tried to kill Jesus as a baby, heard about Him. When Herod heard about Jesus, he said, "This must be John the Baptist come back to life!"

Herod had arrested John and put him in prison because he kept telling Herod it was wrong for him to sleep with his brother's wife, Herodias. Herodias wanted Herod to have John executed, but Herod was afraid of John because he knew John was a good man who followed God. Even when John was in prison, Herod liked to listen to John and hear what he had to say.

That all changed on Herod's birthday, however. Herodias' daughter came and danced for Herod and all the officials at his party. Herod was so pleased by her dancing that he told her, "Ask for anything you want, and even if it is up to half my kingdom, I will give it to you!"

The girl went and asked her mother what she should ask for. Herodias said, "Ask for the head of John the Baptist on a silver platter."

Herodias' daughter went back to Herod and said, "I want the head of John the Baptist, right now, on a platter."

Herod didn't know what to do. He had promised to give her whatever she asked for, but he didn't want to kill John. He decided to keep his word, since if he didn't his guests would know. He sent a soldier to the prison to cut off John's head and bring it up to the party. The girl brought John's head to her mother, and John's followers took his body and buried it.

JESUS FEEDS A HUGE CROWD

MARK 6:30-44; JOHN 6:1-14

Jesus and His disciples went away to a remote place so they could be alone to rest, but the crowds heard where they were going and got there first. When Jesus saw the crowd waiting for Him, He felt sorry for them. Even though He was tired, He taught them and told them many things about God's kingdom.

When it was getting late, some of the disciples said, "Teacher, send these people away so they can go get food. This place is deserted, and it's already late."

"You give them something to eat," Jesus said.

"Don't you know how much that would cost?" the disciples asked. "It would take a whole year's wages!"

Andrew spoke up and said, "I found a young boy who brought some food. He has five small loaves of bread and two fish, but that won't go far with this many people."

"It's enough," Jesus said. "Have the people sit down."

The ground was grassy, so the disciples had the people sit on the grass. There were more than five thousand people. Jesus took the bread, thanked God for it, broke it in pieces, and gave it to the disciples, who passed it around for people to eat. Then He did the same with the fish.

The people ate all they wanted, and the disciples gathered up the leftover pieces so they wouldn't waste anything. The leftovers filled twelve big baskets, even though they had started with only five small loaves and two fish. When the people saw this miraculous sign, they said, "Jesus must be the prophet of God who was promised!"

WALKING ON THE WAVES

MARK 6:45-50; MATTHEW 14:28-33

That night, Jesus told His disciples to cross the lake, but He stayed until the crowds left. During the night, Jesus saw that the disciples were having a hard time trying to fight against the wind and the waves, so He went out to meet them—walking on top of the water! Jesus walked out to the disciples' boat, and He was right next to the boat when they saw Him. At first they thought it must be a ghost! They were so afraid that Jesus said, "It's me, don't worry!"

When Peter heard this, he said, "Lord, if it is really you, tell me to come out to you."

"Come on out!" Jesus said.

Peter climbed out of the boat and stepped onto the waves. He was able to stand! He started walking to Jesus, but then he realized how strong the wind was and how big the waves were. Peter got scared and started sinking. "Save me!" he cried.

Jesus grabbed Peter and helped him up and into the boat. "Why do you have so little faith?" Jesus asked.

The wind and waves died down, and all of the disciples said, "You really are the Son of God."

A FOREIGN WOMAN AND A BLIND MAN

MATTHEW 15:21-28; MARK 8:22-26

Jesus was traveling along the northwest coast in the area called Tyre and Sidon when He met a woman who was a Canaanite. "Lord, Son of David," the woman said, "please help me! My daughter has a demon that is tormenting her."

"I was only sent to reach the lost people of Israel," Jesus said. "They are like sheep without a shepherd."

"Please, Lord," she pleaded.

"It wouldn't be right to take the food that belongs to the children and give it to the dogs," Jesus answered.

"But even the dogs get the scraps that fall under the table," the woman said.

"You have a lot of faith," Jesus said. "You will have what you asked for." That very moment, the woman's daughter was healed.

Another time, some people begged Jesus to heal a blind man. Jesus took the man outside the busy town, then touched his eyes and asked him if he could see. "I see some shapes like trees walking around," the man said. Jesus touched the man's eyes again and he could see clearly. His eyes had been completely healed.

"You can go home now," Jesus said, "but don't go through the town. I don't want to cause a scene." Jesus didn't want people to follow Him just because of the miracles He did. He wanted people to follow Him and listen to His teaching as He taught them how to love God. He wanted them to follow Him because He was the Savior God had promised who would make everything right again between God and His people.

WHO IS JESUS?

MATTHEW 16:13-19

People were saying all sorts of things about Jesus. "What have you heard people saying?" Jesus asked.

"Some people are saying that you are John the Baptist come back to life, or some think you are a prophet from the past, or even the prophet who God promised to send," the disciples asked.

"What about you?" Jesus asked. "What do you believe?"

"You are the Messiah, the chosen one, the Son of God!" Peter said.

"You are blessed, Simon Peter!" Jesus said. "God showed you this. I will call you Peter because your words are the rock on which I will build my church. I will give you the keys of the kingdom of heaven, and God will use you in amazing ways! Anything you lock up on earth will be locked up in heaven, and anything you open on earth will be open in heaven."

A HEAVENLY MEETING

LUKE 9:28-36

A few days later, Jesus took Peter, James, and John up on a mountain with Him to pray. While they were there, Jesus' clothes and face changed and became bright, shining white. Moses and Elijah appeared in shining glory from heaven and talked with Jesus.

The disciples had been sleeping, but when they woke up they saw Jesus in His shining glory with Moses and Elijah. When the heavenly visitors were about to leave, Peter said, "Teacher, it's a good thing we're here! Let's make three shelters, one for each of you!" He didn't really know what he was saying because he was so overwhelmed by what he had seen.

While Peter was still talking, a cloud appeared and the disciples were afraid. A voice came from the cloud and said, "This is my chosen Son. Listen to Him!" After the voice had spoken, the cloud went away, and only Jesus remained. The disciples didn't say anything about what they had seen until much later.

MORE TEACHING AND HEALING

MATTHEW 18:1-20; LUKE 17:11-19

After this, the disciples asked Jesus who would be the greatest in the kingdom of heaven. Jesus brought a young child over and said, "Unless you become like this little child, you will never get into the kingdom of heaven. But if you are humble like this child, not worried about position or fame and trusting completely in me, you will be great in the kingdom of heaven. If you welcome a little child in my name, you welcome me.

It would be terrible for anyone who led one of my followers into sin. It would be better for that person to have a heavy stone tied around his neck and be thrown into the ocean.

"If you have a hand or foot that causes you to sin, you should be willing to cut it off and throw it away rather than keep sinning! It is better to be crippled or lame and still have eternal life than to have all your limbs and be thrown into the fires of hell. If your eye causes you to sin be willing to poke it out instead of sinning more!

"Be kind to these little ones. My Father in heaven loves them. If you had a hundred sheep and one went missing, wouldn't you leave the other ninety-nine sheep while you went looking for the one that was missing? That's how your Father in heaven feels about these little ones. He doesn't want any of them to be lost."

Another time, Jesus was teaching His disciples and He said, "Don't argue among yourselves. If you have disagreements with your brothers and sisters, work it out with them in private or with the other believers. God wants to give you whatever you ask Him when two of you agree. Whenever there are two or three of you together in my name and doing my will, I will be there with you."

When Jesus was on His way to Jerusalem, He met ten men who had a skin disease that caused them to stay far away from any other people and they couldn't even go into a town. They stood a little way off and called out, "Jesus, please have pity on us!"

"Go show yourselves to the priests," Jesus said.

The men went to do what Jesus told them, and on the way, they were healed! When they realized this, one of the men went back and bowed down at Jesus' feet, shouting praises to God. That man was a Samaritan. "Weren't there ten men?" Jesus asked. "What happened to the other nine who were healed? Is this Samaritan the only one who wants to thank God?" Then Jesus told the man, "Go home. Your faith has made you well."

THE FIRST STONE
JOHN 8:1-11

Jesus was teaching in the temple when a group of Pharisees and legal experts dragged a woman in front of the crowd. They said, "Teacher, we caught this woman sleeping with a man she isn't married to. The Law of Moses tells us to kill women like this by throwing stones at her. What do you think we should do?" They were asking Jesus this because they were hoping to trick Him into saying something against the Law.

Jesus didn't answer right away. Instead, He bent down and wrote on the ground with His finger. They kept pestering Him to answer them, so Jesus stood up and said, "If anyone has never sinned, that person will throw the first stone at her." After He said this, Jesus bent down and kept writing.

The people started to leave one by one, starting with the oldest, but then the younger people left too. Eventually Jesus and the woman were left alone.

"Where did they go?" Jesus asked. "Didn't anyone stay to accuse you?"

"No one, Sir," she answered.

"Then I don't accuse you either," Jesus said. "You can go home, but don't sin anymore."

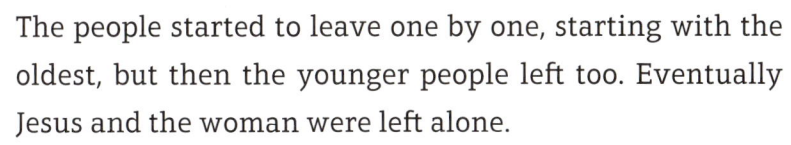

THE GOOD SAMARITAN

LUKE 10:25-37

"Teacher," a legal expert asked one day, "how do I get eternal life?"

"What do the Scriptures say?" Jesus answered.

"Love the Lord your God with all your heart, soul, strength, and mind," the man answered. "They also say to love your neighbor as much as you love yourself."

Jesus said, "That's right. If you do these things, you will have eternal life."

"But who is my neighbor?" the man asked, trying to find a way to make himself look good.

Jesus answered by telling a story:

"There was a man traveling from Jerusalem to Jericho. Some robbers attacked him and beat him until he was almost dead. They took everything he had and left him on the side of the road. A priest walked that way, and he saw the man lying there. When he got close, he walked past on the other side of the road. Later, a temple worker came by, but he also went by on the opposite side from the man who had been robbed."

"A Samaritan was traveling along the road, and when he saw the man, he felt sorry for him. He went over and treated the man's injuries

with ointment, put him on his own donkey, and took him to an inn. The next morning, the Samaritan gave the innkeeper some money and said, 'Please take care of this man. If you need more money, I will give it to you when I return.'"

"Which of these men was a neighbor to the man who was robbed?" Jesus asked.

"The one who showed him pity," the legal expert said.

"Go and do the same thing," Jesus said.

WHAT MATTERS MORE?
LUKE 10:38-42

Jesus was visiting his friends Martha and Mary in a village near Jerusalem. Martha was cooking and cleaning and waiting on everyone, but Mary was just sitting next to Jesus and listening to Him. Martha was stressed, so she went up to Jesus and said, "Lord, don't you see how much I have to do? Tell my sister to help me!"

Jesus answered, "Martha, you are worried about a lot of things, but only one thing is the most important. Mary has chosen to listen to me, and that is the most important thing. I won't take it away from her."

THE GOOD SHEPHERD
JOHN 10:11-18

One time when Jesus was teaching, He said, "I am the good shepherd who gives up His life for the sheep. Hired workers don't care about the sheep like the shepherd does. When they see a wolf, they don't protect the sheep because they don't own them or care about them. They only want to protect themselves, so they run away and let the wolf scatter the whole flock. I am the good shepherd. I know my sheep and my sheep know me. I have other sheep that are not from this sheep pen, and I will bring them in too. Then you will all be one flock with one shepherd. My Father loves me because I give up my life for my sheep. I lay it down willingly so that I can receive it back again. I am doing this because my Father has told me to do it this way.

JESUS' FRIEND LAZARUS
JOHN 11:1-44

Martha and Mary's brother Lazarus was Jesus' friend, too. One day, they sent a message to Jesus and told Him that Lazarus was sick. When Jesus and His disciples finally got to Bethany, the town where Mary, Martha, and Lazarus lived, Lazarus was dead. He had already been in the tomb for four days.

Martha went out to meet Jesus. "Lord, if you had been here, my brother would not have died," she said.

"I am the one who raises the dead," Jesus told her. "Anyone who believes in me will live, even if they die. Do you believe this?"

"Yes, Lord," Martha said, "I believe that you are the Messiah, the Son of God!"

Mary came out as well, and she said, "Lord, if you had been here, my brother would not have died."

Jesus saw how upset Mary was, so He asked, "Where did you bury him?"

"Come and see," she said.

On the way to the tomb, Jesus started crying. The people with Him said, "He must have really loved Lazarus."

When they got to the tomb, there was a large stone in front of the entrance. Jesus told them to roll the stone away, but Martha said, "Lord, by now there will be a terrible smell; he's been in there four days."

Jesus insisted, so they rolled the stone back. Then Jesus looked up to heaven and said, "Father, I know you always answer my prayers. Thank you for answering me so these people will

believe that you sent me." When He was done praying, Jesus said, "Lazarus, come out!"

Lazarus came walking out of the tomb—covered in strips of cloth. They untied him, and they were overjoyed to have their brother and friend back.

STORIES ABOUT GOD'S LOVE FOR LOST PEOPLE

Some experts of the Law complained about Jesus spending time with people they thought were horrible sinners and bad people. "Why is He so friendly with sinners?" they asked.

Jesus said, "If you had a hundred sheep and one of them was missing, wouldn't you leave the other ninety-nine and search for the missing sheep until you found it? And when you did, you would bring it home and call your friends to celebrate with you. In the same way, there is more rejoicing in heaven over one sinner who comes to God than over ninety-nine good people who don't need to repent.

"Suppose a woman had ten silver coins. If she lost one, wouldn't she light a lamp and search her house carefully until she found it? And when she did, she would call her friends and neighbors to celebrate with her. In the same way, God's angels rejoice when even one person comes to God.

"A man had two sons. The younger son told his father, 'Give me my share of the inheritance now!' The father divided his property between his sons, and the younger son took everything he had to a distant country. While he was there, he wasted his money on sinful living until he had nothing left. Then a bad famine spread across the land so that he had nothing to eat.

"He found work feeding pigs, and he was so hungry that he would have been happy to eat the pigs' slop. Finally, he came to his senses and said to himself, 'My father's workers have plenty of food. What am I doing here starving to death? I'll go back to my father and tell him, "Father, I have sinned against God and against you. I am not worthy to be called your son anymore. Please hire me and treat me like one of your workers."'

"The younger son got up and started the long journey home. While he was still far off, his father saw him and felt sorry for him. He ran to his son and hugged him and kissed him.

"The son said, 'Father, I have sinned against God and against you. I am not worthy to be called your son anymore.'

"But his father told his servants, 'Bring my best clothes and put them on him. Give him a ring and sandals. Go kill the best calf and cook it so we can have a feast. My son was dead, but now he is alive again! He was lost, but now he has been found!' So they began to celebrate.

"The older son had been working in the field, and when he came home he asked the servants, 'What's all the noise about?'

"'Your brother is home,' the servants answered, 'and your father has ordered us to prepare a feast to celebrate his safe return.'

"The older brother was so angry that he refused to go into the house. His father came out and asked him to join the party, but he said, 'I have worked for you like a slave for years, and I have always obeyed you. But you never even gave me a small goat so I could have a dinner with my friends. Now this other son of yours, who wasted your money on prostitutes, comes home and you throw him a feast!'

"His father replied, 'My son, you are always with me, and everything I have is yours. We should be happy and celebrate! Your brother was dead, and now he is alive. He was lost, and now he is found.'"

JESUS TEACHES ABOUT MONEY
LUKE 16:10-14, 19-31

Jesus said, "If you can trust someone with little things, you can also trust him with more important matters. But if someone is dishonest about little things, he will be dishonest about important things, too. If you cannot be trusted with money, how will you be trusted with things of real value? Spiritual things are more important than money or things of this world. If you can't be trusted with those things, why should you be trusted with the kingdom of God? You cannot serve two masters. You will like one more than the other or you will be more loyal to one than the other. You cannot serve both God and money."

The Pharisees loved money, so they mocked Jesus for saying this. But Jesus said, "There was a rich man who had only the best clothes and food.

A poor man named Lazarus begged outside his house every day. Lazarus was happy if he could have the scraps of food that fell off the rich man's table. The poor man died, and angels took him to be with Abraham. The rich man also died and was buried. He went to hell, where he suffered terribly. When he looked up and saw Lazarus with Abraham far away, he said, 'Abraham, have pity on me! Send Lazarus to bring me a little water and give me some relief from this fire.'

"Abraham answered, 'Friend, don't you remember that you had everything you wanted while you were alive, and Lazarus was miserable? Now it's the other way around. Besides, there is no way anyone can cross over from one side to the other.'

"The rich man said, 'Can you please send Lazarus to my father's house? Warn my five brothers so they don't come here!'

"Abraham said, 'Your brothers can read what Moses and the prophets wrote. They should listen to it.'

"'That's not enough,' the rich man said, 'but if someone came back from the dead, they would turn to God!'

"'If they won't pay attention to Moses and the prophets,' Abraham said, 'they wouldn't listen even if someone came back from the dead.'"

KEEP PRAYING!
LUKE 18:1-8

Jesus told His disciples a story to encourage them not to give up when they were praying. He said, "There was a judge who did not fear God or care about people. In his town, there was a widow who kept coming to him and insisting he give her fair treatment in court. At first, the judge refused to listen, but finally he said, 'I will help this widow out so she will stop bothering me.'

"God is better than an unfair judge. Won't He help those who pray to Him constantly? He will surely help them right away. Have faith and don't give up! When the Son of Man comes, will He find people who have faith on the earth, who pray and don't give up?"

JESUS LOVES FAMILIES
MARK 10:1-9, 13-16

Some of the Pharisees wanted to test Jesus, so they asked Him if it was right for a man to divorce his wife. "What did Moses say about that?" Jesus asked them.

"Moses let men write up divorce papers and send their wives away," they answered.

"Moses gave you that law because you are so cruel," Jesus said. "When God made the first man and the first woman, He said that when two people get married, they become joined together as if they were one person. No one should separate what God has joined together."

Another time some parents brought their children to see Jesus and have Him bless them. But His disciples told them not to bother their Teacher. Jesus was angry with His disciples. "Let the children come to me!" He said. "God's kingdom belongs to people like these little children, and unless you accept God's kingdom like a little child you will not get in." So, Jesus hugged the children and blessed them.

MORE LESSONS ABOUT MONEY
MATTHEW 19:16-22; MARK 10:17-31

A young man came to Jesus and said, "Teacher, what good thing do I need to do to have eternal life?"

Jesus said, "Why are you asking me about what is good? Only God is good. If you want eternal life, obey God's commandments."

"Which ones?" the man asked.

"Do not murder. Be faithful to your spouse. Do not steal. Do not tell lies. Respect your father and mother, and love others as much as you love yourself," Jesus answered.

"I've always obeyed all of these," the young man said. "What else do I have to do?"

"If you want to be perfect," Jesus said, "sell everything you own and give your money to the poor so you will have riches in heaven. Then come and follow me."

The young man was sad when he heard this because he was very rich. Jesus told his disciples, "It's hard for rich people to enter God's kingdom! It is easier for a camel to go through the eye of a needle than for a rich person to get into God's kingdom."

"Then how can anyone be saved?" the disciples asked.

Jesus answered, "What is impossible for people is possible for God. God can do anything."

"We left everything to follow you!" Peter said. "What about us?"

Jesus answered, "Anyone who has left behind family or property for me and my good news will be rewarded. I will give them even more than they left behind, but they will also be treated badly by the world because they belong to me and the world hates me. In the world to come, they will have eternal life."

A STORY ABOUT HIRED WORKERS
MATTHEW 20:1-16

Jesus told His disciples another story about God's kingdom. He said, "A man who owned a vineyard went out early in the morning to hire some workers for the day. He told them he would pay them the usual amount for a day's work and sent them to his vineyard. At nine, he saw some people in the marketplace with nothing to do, so he hired them to work in his vineyard, too, telling them he would pay them a fair wage. At noon and at three, he did the same thing. Finally, at five, the man found some other people in the marketplace. He asked, 'Why are you standing around doing nothing?'

"The men answered, 'Because no one hired us.' So the man told them to go work in his vineyard, too.

"That evening, the owner of the vineyard gathered all the workers together to give them their pay. He started with the workers who had arrived last, and he gave them a full day's pay, even though they had only worked for an hour. The workers who had been hired in the morning thought they would get paid more, but the owner paid all the workers the same.

"The workers who had been hired first grumbled. They said, 'Those guys only worked for an hour, and we worked in the sun all day. But you paid them the same amount that you paid us!'

"The owner told them, 'I didn't cheat you, friends. I paid you what we agreed on. Take your money and be happy with it. If I want to be generous and pay them the same as you, don't I have the right to do that? Don't be jealous because of my generosity.'"

Jesus said, "That's how it is in God's kingdom: The first will be last, and the last will be first. God offers His goodness and grace to everyone, regardless of who they are or when they come to Him."

ZACCHAEUS MEETS JESUS
LUKE 19:1-10

Jesus was traveling to Jericho where a man named Zacchaeus lived. Zacchaeus was the head tax collector for the Roman rulers, so he was very rich, and he wanted to see what Jesus was like. Because Zacchaeus was short, he had to climb a tree to see over the crowd. When Jesus got to where Zacchaeus was, He said, "Zacchaeus, come down quickly! I want to be your guest today." Zacchaeus hurried down and welcomed Jesus joyfully.

People started grumbling and complaining. "Zacchaeus is a sinner," they said. "He works for the Romans. Why is Jesus eating with him?"

At dinner, Zacchaeus said, "Lord, I'll give half of my possessions to the poor, and if I have cheated anybody, I will pay back four times the amount."

Jesus said, " Today this man has been saved. He has shown that he has faith. I came to seek and save those who were lost."

A STORY ABOUT WORKING FOR GOD
LUKE 19:11-27

Jesus told the crowds that followed Him another story about God's kingdom. He said, "A man of high rank went to a foreign country to be appointed king and then to return. Before he left, he gave ten of his servants each a sum of money. 'Invest this wisely,' he said. 'Earn more money with it until I return.'

"After the man had been crowned king, he went home and gathered his servants to hear how they had used his money. The first servant said, 'Sir, I earned ten times as much money as you gave me.'

"'Well done!" the king said. 'Because you were trustworthy with that money, you will be in charge of ten cities.'

"The second servant said, 'Sir, with the money you gave me, I was able to earn five times as much.'

"'Well done,' the king said. 'You will be in charge of five cities.'

"One of the servants came forward and said, 'Master, here is your money. I kept it safe for you in a handkerchief. I knew that you are very strict, so I was afraid of you.'

"'You terrible, lazy servant!' the king said. "You knew that I am strict, so you should have at least put my money in the bank. Then, I would have gotten it back with interest.' There were other servants nearby, and the king told them, 'Take his money away and give it to the first servant.'

"'But, Sir,' they said, 'he already has ten times as much!'

"'Whoever uses what he was given will be given more, but whoever does not use what he was given will lose even that."

JESUS RETURNS TO JERUSALEM
JOHN 12:1-8; LUKE 19:28-44; MARK 11:15-19; MATTHEW 21:14-16; MARK 12:41-44

There were six days until the Passover festival, and Jesus visited His friends Mary, Martha, and Lazarus on His way to Jerusalem. Martha prepared a meal and served it to Him. Then Mary took an expensive bottle of perfume and poured it on Jesus' feet. She wiped His feet with her hair, and the whole house smelled like the perfume.

Judas, the disciple who would later betray Jesus, said, "Why didn't she sell that perfume and give the money to the poor?"

He didn't really care about the poor, though. He was the one in charge of the disciples' money, and he sometimes stole from the moneybag.

"Leave her alone!" Jesus said. "She saved this perfume to prepare me for burial. You will always have the poor with you, but I will not always be here."

Jesus sent two of His disciples ahead to the next village and said, "You will see a young donkey that has never been ridden. Untie it and bring it back here. If anyone asks what you're doing, just tell them the Lord needs it."

The disciples found the donkey, just like Jesus had said. When they were untying it, the owners asked, "Why are you taking our donkey?"

"The Lord needs it," the disciples said.

The disciples led the donkey back to Jesus and put clothes on its back so Jesus could ride on it. As He rode along, people began putting clothes down in the road ahead of Him. A huge crowd gathered and started shouting and praising God. "Blessed is the one who comes in the name of the Lord!" they said. "Glory to God!"

Some Pharisees were in the crowd, and they said, "Jesus, tell those people to stop yelling!"

"If they kept quiet, the rocks would start shouting," Jesus answered.

Once He reached Jerusalem, Jesus went to the temple, where He saw people buying and selling animals for sacrifices and exchanging money for a profit. He chased out all of the shoppers and salesmen, then He knocked over the money-changers' tables and the bird cages. He wouldn't let anyone bring their goods into the temple. "The Scriptures say, 'My house is a place of worship for all nations,'" Jesus said. "But you have made it a den of robbers!"

The head priests and the legal experts were enraged by this, and they started looking for a way to kill Jesus. But they were afraid to do anything against Him in public because the crowds loved Him.

Jesus stayed in the temple, and blind and lame people came to Him. He healed them all, but the priests and legal experts were angry. "Don't you hear those children shouting, 'Praise to the Son of David?'" they asked.

"I do," Jesus answered. "Don't you remember that the Scriptures say, 'Small children will sing praises to you?'"

While Jesus was in the temple, He saw people bringing their offerings to the box by the entrance. A lot of rich people gave large amounts of money, but a poor widow came and put in two small coins worth only pennies. Jesus told His disciples, "Do you see that widow? She put in more than anyone else. Everyone else gave money that they didn't need, but she is so poor that she gave the only money she had for food."

A STORY ABOUT TEN BRIDESMAIDS

MATTHEW 25:1-13

While He was in Jerusalem Jesus said, "God's kingdom is like ten brides-maids getting ready for a wedding feast. They took their oil lamps and went to meet the groom. Five of them were wise, but five were foolish. The foolish bridesmaids didn't bring any extra oil for their lamps, but the wise bridesmaids did. The groom was late, so the bridesmaids fell asleep.

"A shout woke them in the middle of the night, 'Here comes the groom!'

"The bridesmaids prepared their lamps. 'Give us some of your oil,' the foolish bridesmaids said. 'Our lamps are going out!'

"'We only have enough for ourselves,' the wise bridesmaids said. 'Go buy some.'

"While they were gone the groom arrived and brought the bridesmaids who were ready into the feast with him. When the others returned, they said, 'Let us in!'

"But the groom answered them, 'I don't know you!'"

"Always be ready," Jesus said. "Because you don't know the time or day that I'll return."

JESUS' LAST SUPPER WITH THE DISCIPLES

MATTHEW 26:1-5, 14-16; LUKE 22:7-14, 24-30; JOHN 13:1-9, 12-17; MARK 14:18-25

After Jesus had finished teaching, He told the disciples, "In two days, it will be the Passover. Then the Son of Man will be taken by His enemies and nailed to a cross."

That same time, the head priests were meeting together to plan how they could secretly arrest Jesus and have Him killed. "We shouldn't do it during Passover," they said, "or the people will turn against us. We need to do it secretly to avoid a riot."

Judas Iscariot, one of the disciples, went to the head priests and asked, "How much will you pay me to help you arrest Jesus?" They paid him thirty silver coins, and he was on the lookout from then on for a way to help the religious leaders arrest Jesus when there were no crowds around.

When the day for Passover arrived, Jesus told Peter and John, "Go and prepare the meal for us."

"Where should we prepare it?" they asked.

"You will see a man in the city carrying a jar of water," Jesus said. "Follow him home and tell the owner of the house, 'Our teacher would like to know if He can celebrate the Passover here.' The owner will take you upstairs and show you a room set up for our meal. Prepare it there. Peter and John did what Jesus said, and they prepared the meal for Jesus and the twelve disciples.

When it was time to eat, some of the disciples were arguing over which of them was the greatest. Jesus said, "You know that rulers like to boss people around, but you shouldn't be like that. The most important person among you should be like a servant. People think the one who is served is more important than the one who serves, but I have been a servant with you. You have all stayed with me through

247

everything, so you will rule with me in God's kingdom. You will eat and drink with me and sit on thrones to judge Israel someday.

Even before the meal, Judas had been influenced by the devil to betray Jesus that night. Jesus knew that He would soon return to His Father, and that everything was in God's hands. During the meal, Jesus got up and took off His outer robe. He wrapped a towel around His waist and put some water in a basin. Then He went to each of His disciples and washed their feet.

When Jesus got to Peter, Peter said, "Lord, are you really going to wash my feet?"

"You don't understand this right now," Jesus said, "but later it will make sense."

"You'll never wash my feet!" Peter said.

"Unless I wash your feet, you don't belong to me," Jesus said.

"Then don't just wash my feet," Peter said. "Wash my head and my hands, too!"

After Jesus had washed all His disciples' feet, He got dressed again and said, "Do you understand what I have done for you? You call me your teacher and Lord, and I am. If I am your teacher and Lord and I have washed your feet, you should be willing to do the same thing for each other. You must follow my example because no servant is greater than his master, and messengers are not more important than the one that sent them. God will bless you if you serve each other."

During dinner, Jesus said, "The person who will betray me is sitting at this table with me right now."

The disciples were shocked and horrified. All of them asked, "You don't mean me, do You?"

"One of you twelve who is eating with me will betray me," Jesus answered. "It has to be this way because the Scriptures say the Son of Man must be given over to sinful men, but it will be terrible for the one who betrays me. It would be better for him if he had never been born."

While they were eating, Jesus took some bread and blessed it. Then He broke it and handed it to His disciples. "This is my body," Jesus said. "Take it and eat it." Then Jesus took a glass of wine and gave it to the disciples and they all drank some. "This is my blood, which is poured out for everyone," Jesus said. "God is making a new covenant with people, a new promise through my blood. From now on, I will not drink wine again until I drink it with you in God's kingdom."

IN THE GARDEN

MARK 14:26-42; JOHN 14:1-6, 17:1-18:11; MATTHEW 26:48-49; LUKE 22:51-53

After dinner, Jesus and His friends sang a hymn together and went out to the garden of Gethsemane on the Mount of Olives, just outside Jerusalem. On the way there, Jesus told them, "You will all run away and reject me, just as it is written, 'I will strike the shepherd and the sheep will scatter.' But once I come back to life, I will meet you in Galilee."

"Even if everyone else abandons you, I never will!" Peter said.

Jesus answered him, "Peter, tonight, before the rooster crows, you will say three times that you don't even know me."

"Even if I had to die with you, I would never deny knowing you!" Peter said, and the other disciples agreed.

As they were walking, Jesus wanted to encourage them, so He said, "Don't be afraid. You believe in God, so have faith in me, too. My Father's house is full of rooms. I am going there to make a place ready for you. When I am done, I will come back and take you with me so that we can be together forever. You know how to get where I am going."

Thomas said, "Lord, you haven't told us where you are going, so how can we know how to get there?"

Jesus said, "I am the way, the truth, and the life! The only way to get to the Father is through me."

When Jesus was done talking to His disciples, He prayed for them. He said, "Father, the time has come to glorify me so I can glorify you. You have given me power to share eternal life with those who are yours, and eternal life is knowing you, the only true God, and me, your only Son whom you sent. These followers of mine have seen what you are like through me, and I have told them everything you wanted them to know. Through me, they have come to know you, and I want them to be together with us. Keep them safe from the evil one and protect them in the truth by the power of my name."

After this prayer, Jesus took Peter, James, and John with Him deeper into the garden and went away to pray some more. He was overwhelmed

with sadness and He told them, "I feel like I am dying from grief. Wait here and stay awake with me."

When He had gone a little further, Jesus knelt down and prayed, "Father! If it is possible, please don't make me suffer this way. But I won't do my own will, only your will."

Jesus went back to Peter, James, and John, and they were fast asleep. "You're sleeping?" He asked. "Couldn't you even stay awake for an hour? Wake up and pray that you will be strong. Your heart wants to do what is right, but your body is weak."

Jesus went away and prayed the same prayer again, and when He returned, they were sleeping again. He went away and returned a third time and said, "You're still asleep, but it's time for the Son of Man to be handed over to evil men. Get up! The one who is betraying me is here."

Judas knew where Jesus was, because Jesus and the disciples met in Gethsemane often. He had agreed to betray Jesus, so he went there with some soldiers and temple guards who had been sent by the religious leaders who hated Jesus. They carried torches and weapons. When Jesus saw them, He said, "Who are you looking for?"

"Jesus of Nazareth," they said.

"I am Jesus," He answered. When He said this, they all fell back in fear, so He asked again, "Who are you looking for?"

"We're looking for Jesus of Nazareth," they said.

"I already told you that I am Jesus," He replied. "If it's me you want, then let the others go."

Now Judas had told the guards that they should arrest the person he kissed so they were sure to get the right man. Judas walked up to Jesus and said, "Hello, teacher," and kissed Him.

"Judas," Jesus said, "are you really going to betray me with a kiss?"

The soldiers moved to arrest Jesus, but Peter had brought a sword with him. He drew the sword and lashed out with it, hitting a man named Malchus and cutting off his ear.

"Put your sword away," Jesus told Peter. "I must do what the Father has given me to do." Then Jesus touched the man's ear and healed it. Turning to the soldiers, Jesus said, "You could have arrested me any day when I was in the temple. Why are you coming out here with torches and clubs to treat me like a criminal who is starting a rebellion? I'll tell you why. It's because you have dark hearts and you love to act in darkness."

And they took Jesus away.

JESUS ON TRIAL

JOHN 18:12-14, 28-19:16; LUKE 22:54-62, LUKE 23:7-12; MARK 14:53-65, 15:1

The Roman soldiers and temple guards took Jesus to the house of the high priest, a man named Caiaphas. When the religious leaders had been trying to figure out what to do about Jesus, Caiaphas had told them, "It's better for one man to die for the sake of the people." He didn't realize it, but Caiaphas had been speaking a prophecy about how Jesus would die in the place of all people to pay the price for their sins.

That night, the other disciples ran away, but Peter followed the soldiers and Jesus at a distance. It was cold, so some people had made a fire in the courtyard of the high priest's house. Peter went and joined them. A servant girl saw Peter and looked at him closely. "This man was with Jesus," she said.

"I don't even know Him!" Peter said.

A little later, someone else said, "You must be one of Jesus' followers."

"I'm not!" Peter insisted.

An hour later, another man said, "No, you must have been with Jesus. You're both from Galilee. I can tell by your accent!"

"I swear that I don't know Him!" Peter said. While he was still talking, a rooster crowed, and Peter remembered that Jesus had told him, "Before the rooster crows, you will deny that you know me three times." Peter ran out of the courtyard, weeping uncontrollably.

Inside the house, the chief priest brought in the whole council of Jewish leaders and teachers of the Law of Moses. They were all trying to find someone who could accuse Jesus of a crime that deserved the death penalty, but they couldn't find anyone. There were many people willing to lie about Jesus, but their stories didn't agree. Finally, the high priest stood up and asked Jesus, "Don't you have something to say for yourself? Don't you hear all these charges they are bringing against you?"

But Jesus didn't say anything.

The high priest asked, "Are you the Messiah, God's chosen one, the Son of God Most High?"

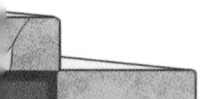

"I am," Jesus said, "and you will see the Son of Man sitting at the right hand of God and coming on the clouds of heaven."

The high priest ripped his robe in anger and said, "We don't need any more witnesses! You heard Him claim to be God with your own ears! What do you think we should do?"

"Put Him to death!" they all shouted.

The people there started hitting Jesus and spitting on Him. The guards blindfolded Him and hit Him, saying, "Prophecy! Tell us who hit you!" In the morning, very early, all the people who had condemned Jesus, the chief priests and teachers of the Law and the whole Jewish council took Jesus to the house of the Roman governor, a man named Pilate.

When Pilate heard that Jesus was from Galilee, he said, "I'm not in charge of Galilee. Isn't Herod in Jerusalem right now? Galilee is his region. Send this man to Herod."

Herod was happy to get a chance to see Jesus, since he had heard so much about Him. He was hoping to see a miracle. Herod asked Jesus a lot of questions, but Jesus didn't answer him, even when the leaders of the people accused Him of all sorts of crimes. Herod and his soldiers mocked Jesus and made fun of Him. They put a fancy robe on Him and sent Him back to Pilate.

Back at Pilate's house, the Jews didn't want to go in, since that would make them unclean and they wouldn't be allowed to celebrate the Passover. Instead, Pilate came out to them and asked, "What has this man done? Why are you bringing Him to me?"

"He calls himself king of the Jews, " the leaders of the people answered.

"Judge Him yourself, then," Pilate said.

"We aren't allowed to crucify anyone," the leaders said. "Only you have that authority."

Pilate took Jesus inside to question Him. "Are you the king of the Jews?" Pilate asked.

"Is this your own question, or did someone tell you to ask that?" Jesus said.

"I'm not a Jew," Pilate answered. "Your own people brought you to me. What crime have you committed?"

"My kingdom is not of this world," Jesus said. "If it were, my followers would have fought to save me from the Jewish leaders. No, my kingdom is different from any kingdom in this world."

"So you are a king?" Pilate asked.

"You said it yourself. I am," Jesus said. "I was born and came into this world to speak the truth. Everyone who belongs to the truth hears my voice."

"What is truth?" Pilate asked, turning to go back outside.

Pilate took Jesus out to the crowd and said, "This man hasn't committed any crime! Here's what I'll do. I usually release a prisoner for you during your festival. Shall I release the king of the Jews?"

"No!" the crowd shouted. "We don't want Him! Give us Barabbas." Barabbas was a leader of a rebellion who had killed a lot of people in an uprising against Rome.

Pilate ordered his soldiers to whip Jesus. Then the soldiers made a crown out of thorny branches and put it on His head. They put a purple robe on Him and mocked Him, saying, "Look, the king of the Jews!" And they beat Him with their fists.

Pilate brought Jesus out to the crowd again and said, "Here is the man! Look, you can see for yourselves that I have found Him innocent."

As soon as they saw Jesus, the leaders of the people shouted, "Crucify Him! Crucify! Crucify!"

"You take Him and crucify Him," Pilate said. "I don't see any reason to punish Him."

"He claimed to be God's Son," the leaders of the crowd answered. "Our Law says that He must die!"

Pilate was afraid when he heard this. He took Jesus back inside and asked, "Where are you from?"

Jesus didn't answer.

"Why won't you answer me?" Pilate asked. "Don't you know that I have the power to set you free or have you killed?"

"You would not have any power over me unless God gave it to you," Jesus answered. "Because of this, the one who handed me over to you did the worse thing."

Pilate appealed to the Jewish leaders one last time to set Jesus free, but when he tried to speak to the crowd, they shouted, "If you let that man go free, you aren't a friend of the emperor! Anyone who claims to be a king is the emperor's enemy."

Pilate brought Jesus out to the crowd one last time and said, "Look at your king!"

"KILL HIM!" the crowd shouted. "Crucify Him! Nail Him to a cross!"

"You want me to crucify your king?" Pilate asked.

"We have no king besides the emperor!" the people answered.

So Pilate gave in to the crowd and handed Jesus over to be crucified.

JESUS DIES FOR OUR SINS

LUKE 23:26-44; JOHN 19:28-30; MATTHEW 27:51-54

The soldiers led Jesus out of the city. Jesus was struggling to carry the heavy cross, so the soldiers grabbed a man named Simon who was passing by and made him help Jesus carry the cross out to the place called Golgotha, which means "Skull Hill." A lot of people were following Jesus to see what would happen. Some women who had followed Him wept when they saw Him

pass by. Jesus told them, "Don't cry for me, women of Jerusalem. Cry for yourselves and your children. There is a time coming that will be even more terrible. If they are willing to do this to me now, when I did nothing wrong, what else will they be willing to do later to the rest of you?"

When they reached Golgotha, the soldiers nailed Jesus to the cross by His hands and feet and raised Him up. "Father, forgive them!" Jesus said. "They don't know what they're doing."

The soldiers took Jesus' clothes and divided them among themselves. They gambled for His robe because it was all one piece and they didn't want to tear it. The leaders of the people mocked Jesus, saying, "If He is

really God's chosen one, let Him save Himself! He saved others, but He can't save Himself!"

Pilate had ordered the soldiers to hang a sign above Jesus that said, "This is the King of the Jews." The soldiers said, "If you are the King of the Jews, save yourself!"

Two criminals were also crucified next to Jesus, one on either side. One of the criminals joined in the mocking. He said, "Aren't you the Messiah? Save yourself! And save us, too!"

But the other criminal said, "Don't you have any fear of God, even while we're dying? Here we are, dying side by side, but you're mocking Him. We deserve to die, but He didn't do anything wrong!" He turned to Jesus and said, "Please remember me when you enter your kingdom."

Jesus told him, "I promise, today you will be with me in paradise."

At noon, the sky got as dark as night, and it was dark for several hours. Jesus knew that He had accomplished what God had sent Him to do. He wanted to fulfill what the Scriptures said about Him, so He said, "I'm thirsty!" One of the soldiers dipped a sponge on a stick in sour wine and gave it to Jesus. After Jesus tasted the sour wine, He said, "It is finished!" Then He bowed His head and died.

Right away, the thick curtain in the temple was torn in half from top to bottom, and a huge earthquake shook the ground and broke rocks apart. Graves even opened, and some of God's people came back to life. When the soldiers guarding Jesus saw what happened, they said, "He really was the Son of God!"

It seemed like all was lost, but this was not the end. Jesus' death would make it possible for people to have a relationship with God again.

267

BURIED IN A BORROWED TOMB

JOHN 19:31-34; MATTHEW 27:57-66

The next day was the Passover Sabbath so the Jewish leaders didn't want the bodies to stay up on the crosses overnight. Pilate ordered the soldiers to break the men's legs so they would die faster, and the soldiers broke the legs of the two criminals. But when the soldiers got to Jesus, they saw that He was already dead. Instead of breaking His legs, they stabbed Him in the side with a spear to see if He was really dead. When they did, water and blood came out, which showed that He was really and truly dead.

That evening, one of Jesus' followers named Joseph asked Pilate for Jesus' body. Pilate ordered the soldiers to give it to Joseph, and Joseph took it and wrapped it up in burial cloths. Then Joseph took Jesus' body and laid it in his own tomb that had been cut out of solid rock. Joseph rolled a large stone in front of the entrance and went away. Mary and Mary Magdalene were there with Joseph.

The next day, the Jewish leaders told Pilate, "Before He died, this man said that He would come back to life in three days. Please have some soldiers guard the tomb so His followers don't come and steal the body. Otherwise, they may lie and tell people He has come back to life." Pilate agreed, and ordered some soldiers to seal the tomb and stand guard.

HE'S ALIVE!

MATTHEW 28:1-10; JOHN 20:2-29; LUKE 24:37-45

On the day after the Sabbath, the third day since Jesus had died, Mary and Mary Magdalene got up early in the morning to go see the tomb. When they were on their way, a strong earthquake shook the ground. An angel appeared from God. He rolled away the heavy stone and sat on it. The angel was so bright that his clothes looked like lightning, and the guards were so afraid that they fainted and lay on the ground like they were dead.

When the women arrived, they saw the angel. He said, "Don't be afraid! You are looking for Jesus, who was crucified. He isn't here! He has risen, just like He said! Come and see where His body used to be." The women looked in the tomb and saw that it was empty. "Now go and tell His

disciples that He is alive again and will meet them in Galilee," the angel said. "Hurry and tell them to meet Him there!"

The women were scared, but they were also filled with joy as they ran to tell the disciples what they had seen. When they arrived, the women told the disciples, "Jesus's body is gone from the tomb!"

Peter and John ran as fast as they could to the tomb, and Mary Magdalene followed them. John got there first, but he just stood outside, looking in at the burial cloth lying in the empty tomb. When Peter got there, he went right into the tomb. The burial cloths were lying on the ground, but the cloth that had been over Jesus' face was rolled up by itself. Peter and John didn't realize that the Scriptures had already promised Jesus would come back to life, but when they saw the empty tomb, they believed. They went back to tell the other disciples what they had seen.

Mary Magdalene was still standing outside the tomb, crying, when she looked inside and saw two angels sitting where Jesus's body had been. "Why are you crying?" the angels asked her.

"Someone has taken my Lord away, and I don't know where they put Him!" she answered.

After she said this, she turned around and saw Jesus standing behind her, but she didn't recognize Him. Jesus asked, "Why are you crying? Who are you looking for?"

Mary thought He was a gardener and said, "Sir, if you have moved His body, please tell me where He is so I can go get Him."

"Mary," Jesus said.

When He said her name, Mary recognized that it was Jesus. "Teacher!" she said.

"Don't hold on to me," Jesus said. "I haven't returned to my Father yet. Go and tell my disciples that I am returning to my Father and their Father, to my God and their God." Mary went away and told the disciples that she had seen Jesus.

That same evening, the disciples were all gathered together in a locked room because they were afraid the Jewish leaders would want to kill them, too. Jesus suddenly appeared in the middle of the room with them.

"Peace be with you," Jesus said.

The disciples were afraid because they thought He was a ghost.

"Why are you frightened?" Jesus asked. "Why are you doubting? Look at the scars in my hands and feet! Touch me and see for yourselves that it's really me. Ghosts don't have flesh and bones like I do. Jesus showed them the nail marks in His hands and feet and ate some food to show them that He was no ghost or spirit. They were all overcome with joy and so amazed that they could hardly believe it was really Him.

"Don't you understand?" Jesus asked. "While I was with you, I told you that all of the things written about me by Moses and the Prophets had to come true." Then He explained the Scriptures to them and helped them understand. When He was finished, Jesus said, "I am sending you out into the world like the Father has sent me. You will receive the Holy Spirit, and if you forgive anyone's sins, God will forgive them, too."

Thomas hadn't been there when Jesus appeared to the other disciples, so when they told him, "We have seen the Lord!" he replied, "I can't believe it unless I see the nail scars in His hands and touch them myself. I want to put my hand in His side where the spear was. Only then would I be able to believe!"

A week later, the disciples were together in the same room again, and Thomas was with them. Suddenly, Jesus came in even though the doors were locked and stood in the middle of the room. He greeted all of the

disciples and told Thomas, "Put your finger here. Look at the scars in my hands. Put your hand in my side. Don't doubt anymore. Have faith!"

Thomas bowed down and said, "You are my Lord and my God!"

Jesus told him, "You have faith because you have seen me. But the people who have faith without seeing me will be even more blessed!"

BREAKFAST BY THE SEA

JOHN 21:1-19

Some of Jesus' disciples had gone to Galilee, to go fishing on the Sea of Galilee. Peter was there with Thomas, Nathanael, James, John, and two others. They were out in a boat all night fishing, but they hadn't caught anything. Early in the morning, Jesus appeared on the shore, but the disciples didn't recognize Him from so far away. He shouted to them, "Have you caught anything, my friends?"

"No!" they answered.

"Put your nets down on the other side of your boat," Jesus told them.

They did what He said, and their net was so full that they couldn't even haul it into the boat. Then John realized it was Jesus on the shore. He told Peter, "It's the Lord!" Peter jumped out of the boat while the other disciples dragged the net full of fish back with them.

When the disciples got out of the boat, Jesus was waiting for them with some bread and a small fire with some fish on it. "Bring some of your fish over," He said. Peter waded ashore, dragging the net with him. There were a lot of big fish in the net, but it hadn't ripped.

"Come and eat!" Jesus told them. He took some of the bread and gave it to the disciples, then He did the same with the fish.

When they had finished eating, Jesus asked Peter, "Simon son of John, do you love me more than these others?"

"Lord, you know I do!" Simon Peter answered.

274

"Feed my lambs," Jesus said. Then a second time, Jesus asked, "Simon son of John, do you love me?"

"Yes, Lord," Peter answered. "You know I love you!"

"Take care of my sheep," Jesus said. Finally, a third time, Jesus asked, "Simon son of John, do you love me?"

Peter was hurt that Jesus had asked three times if he loved Him. He answered, "Lord, you know everything. You know that I love you."

"Feed my sheep," Jesus said. "When you were a young man, you dressed yourself and went wherever you wanted, but when you are old, others will dress you and will lead you where you don't want to go." Jesus told him this to show Peter how he would bring honor to God in his death. Then He said, "Follow me!"

THE BEGINNING OF THE CHURCH
ACTS 1:3-11; 2:1-47

Jesus met with His disciples many times over the course of forty days after He rose from the dead. He taught them more about God's kingdom and helped them get ready for when He would leave them and go back to heaven. "Stay in Jerusalem for now," He said. "My Father will send you the Holy Spirit, just like I promised. When the Holy Spirit comes, He will give you power, and you will be my witnesses, telling people about me in Jerusalem, in the rest of Judea, in Samaria, and all over the world." When He had finished speaking, Jesus rose up into the sky. He passed into a cloud, and they couldn't see Him anymore.

The disciples kept looking up in the sky, but Jesus was gone. He had returned to heaven.

Two angels appeared next to the disciples and said, "Why are you standing here, looking up at the sky? Jesus has gone up into heaven, but He will come back the same way that you saw Him leave."

277

On the day of the festival called Pentecost, all the disciples were gathered together in one room, and a loud noise like the wind of a mighty storm came from heaven and filled the whole house. The disciples looked at each other and saw something that looked like little flames moving around and coming to rest on each person. Then the Holy Spirit filled them all, and they were able to speak in other languages that they didn't even know.

There were Jews from all over the world in Jerusalem for the festival, and when they heard the loud sound, a big crowd of them gathered around the house where the disciples were. The people in the crowd were surprised, because they heard the disciples speaking to them in their own native languages. They said, "Aren't all of these people from Galilee? How can they speak to us in languages we understand? Some of us are from places that are far away and we speak all kinds of different languages. Some of us were born Jewish and others converted from other religions. But all of us can understand these people using our own languages to tell us about the wonders of God!"

Many people were excited to hear the disciples speaking in their languages, but others made fun of them. "They're drunk," they said.

Peter stood up in front of the crowd with the rest of the apostles, and said, "Friends, visitors, everyone in Jerusalem, listen to me! We are not drunk! It is only nine o'clock in the morning, after all. What you are seeing and hearing is what God promised through the prophet Joel, who said, 'In the last days, I will give my Spirit to everyone, from the least to the greatest, and they will all speak in my name.' He has sent us to tell you the good news about His Son, Jesus of Nazareth, whom you killed, but who rose again and is now seated next to God in heaven."

Many people believed that Jesus was God's Son after they heard the apostles' message, and others saw them perform miracles like those Jesus had done. Three thousand people believed in just the first day! Everyone who saw the miraculous signs was amazed, and the number of people who believed and followed Jesus grew every day. All of the new believers lived together in Jerusalem, sharing everything they had with one another and listening to the teaching of the apostles.

TROUBLE FOR THE CHURCH
ACTS 3:1-4:22; 5:12-42; 6:8-7:60

One day, Peter and John were on their way to the temple to pray. There was a man by the door who had been unable to walk his whole life. When this man saw Peter and John entering the temple, he asked them for money.

"Look at me," Peter said, and the man looked at him, expecting some sort of handout. "I don't have any money," Peter continued, "but I will give you what I do have. In the name of Jesus Christ, get up and walk." Peter took the man by the hand and helped him up. Right away, the man's legs and ankles were healed and became strong, and he was able to walk. He followed Peter and John into the temple, leaping in the air and praising God.

A crowd gathered to see the man who had been healed. Peter spoke to the crowd in a place called Solomon's Porch. He said, "My friends, why are you surprised about what has happened? It is not because we are special that this man was healed. The God of our ancestors, Abraham, Isaac, and Jacob, has done this to bring glory to His Son and Servant, Jesus of Nazareth. He is the very person you betrayed by bringing Him to the governor and demanding His death, even though Pilate wanted to set Him free.

"You killed Jesus, the one who brings life, but God raised Him from the dead. We can all tell you about Him and what He has done. This man who used to be crippled had faith in the name of Jesus, and that faith is what made him whole. Jesus healed him so that you could see His power."

While Peter and John were still talking, a group of priests and Sadducees came in with the temple guards. The Sadducees were upset because they didn't believe it was possible for anyone to rise from the dead, and Peter and John were teaching people that Jesus had done just that. The temple guards arrested Peter and John and put them in prison. But many of the people who had heard their message believed in Jesus.

The next morning, the Jewish leaders and the teachers of the Law of Moses gathered together to question Peter and John. They brought them from the prison and had them stand in front of the whole assembly. "By whose power and authority have you performed this miraculous healing?" the leaders asked.

Peter began to speak, and the Holy Spirit filled him and told him what to say. He said, "You are asking us about the good deed we did by healing a crippled man, but I have something more important I need to tell you. This man was healed and is standing here completely well because of the power of Jesus Christ of Nazareth! You killed Jesus by having Him crucified, but God raised Him from the dead. Jesus is the only one with the power to save people from their sins! His name is the only name in the whole world that can save."

The leaders and teachers were amazed at Peter and John and how bravely they were able to speak in front of the assembly. They knew that they were both ordinary men, not scholars or experts in the Law. The leaders had them leave the room so they could decide what to do. "Everyone in the city knows what these men did," the leaders said. "What can we do? We can't pretend it didn't happen." When they called Peter and John back in, the leaders told them not to teach anyone about Jesus anymore.

Peter and John answered, "Should we obey you or God? We cannot be silent about what we have seen."

The leaders couldn't find an excuse to punish Peter and John so they warned them again not to teach people about Jesus and let them go.

After that, the apostles met with the other believers and prayed for boldness to tell others about Jesus. After their prayer, the entire house they were meeting in shook with God's power. A lot of people had begun to believe in Jesus, and the priests and Sadducees were jealous of the apostles. They arrested the apostles and put them in prison. That night, an angel came and opened the doors of the prison. He led the apostles out and said, "Go back to the temple and tell everyone how to have new life in Jesus."

The apostles went to the temple right away, even though it was before dawn. They started teaching anyone who would listen. When the high priest sent guards to the prison to bring the apostles in front of the council of Jewish leaders, the guards came back alone. "The prison doors are locked," they said, "but there was no one inside."

A messenger rushed in and said, "Those men you arrested are in the temple right now! They are teaching people about Jesus!"

The guards went and brought the apostles to the council, but they didn't use force, because they were afraid the people might turn against them if they did. When the apostles were all gathered before the council, the high priest said, "Didn't we order you not to teach people about Jesus? But you have been teaching people about Him all over Jerusalem, and you're even blaming us for killing Him."

Peter spoke for the apostles. He said, "We obey God, not people. And you did kill Jesus by nailing Him to a cross. But God, the God of our ancestors, raised Him from the dead and made Him our Lord and Savior. God has given Him a place of power and glory by His right hand, so that the people of Israel will turn to Him and receive forgiveness for their sins. We are telling you about these things, and the Holy Spirit is speaking through us. He is God's gift to everyone who believes God and obeys Him."

When the members of the council heard what Peter said, some of them got so angry that they wanted to kill the apostles. One of the Pharisees, a respected teacher named Gamaliel, had the guards take the apostles out of the room so he could talk to the council. He said, "People of Israel, watch out that you don't make a mistake in how you treat these men. If what they are doing is their own idea, then it will fail. But if God is behind it, nothing you do will be able to stop them. Leave them alone, unless you want to fight against God."

The council all agreed with Gamaliel, so they called the apostles back in. They had them whipped and warned them not to teach people about Jesus. Then they let them go. When the apostles left the council, they weren't upset about their punishment. They were happy that God had let them suffer for Jesus and His message. They spent all their time teaching people about Jesus in the temple and in people's homes, and they never stopped telling everyone the good news that Jesus was the promised Messiah.

One of the new believers was a man named Stephen. God gave Stephen the power to perform miracles, but some of the Jewish people from outside of Jerusalem started to argue with him. These men couldn't beat Stephen in an argument, and they were upset. They hired some people to lie about Stephen and say that he had said horrible things about Moses and God that, according to the Law, had the punishment of death. Then they dragged Stephen in front of the council and accused him of claiming that Jesus would destroy the temple and change all of their religious traditions.

When the high priest asked Stephen if the accusers were telling the truth, he said, "You are just like your ancestors. You always fight against the Holy Spirit. Your ancestors mistreated and killed the prophets who told them about the coming of God's chosen one, and now you have killed Jesus, the Messiah."

The council members were so angry after Stephen's speech that they wanted to kill him. Stephen looked up and said, "I see heaven open, and the Son of Man is standing at God's right hand!"

The council members covered their ears and shouted for Stephen to be quiet. They dragged him outside the city and stoned him to death. As Stephen was dying, he said, "Lord Jesus, please receive my spirit! Don't blame them for what they are doing."

SAUL MEETS JESUS
ACTS 8:1-3; 9:1-18

After Stephen died, there was a time of great suffering and persecution for the church in Jerusalem. All of the believers besides the apostles had to run away. They were scattered across the rest of Judea and Samaria. A man named Saul was one of the biggest troublemakers for the church. He went around arresting people for believing in Jesus and throwing them in prison.

Saul got a letter from the high priest to the Jewish leaders in the city of Damascus that gave him permission to arrest any believers in Jesus that he found there. As Saul was traveling to Damascus, a bright light from heaven suddenly appeared all around him. Saul fell to the ground, and he heard a voice say, "Saul, Saul, why are you persecuting me?"

"Who are you?" Saul asked.

"I am Jesus," the voice answered, "the one you keep attacking. Get up and go into the city. Someone there will tell you what to do."

The people with Saul had heard the voice, but they hadn't seen the light. When Saul got up, he was blind. His companions had to lead him by the hand the rest of the way to Damascus.

In Damascus, there lived a believer named Ananias. Jesus spoke to him in a vision. "Ananias," Jesus said, "go to Judas' house on Straight Street. There is a man there named Saul of Tarsus."

"Lord," Ananias said, "I have heard about that man. He has done horrible things to your followers in Jerusalem."

"Go to him," Jesus said. "I have chosen him to be my messenger. He will tell foreigners and kings about me, and he will suffer for me and my message."

Ananias obeyed and went to the house where Saul was staying. He said, "Saul, the Lord Jesus sent me to you. He is the one who appeared to you on the road. He will restore your sight and give you the Holy Spirit."

Right away, something like scales fell off Saul's eyes and he could see again. He got up and Ananias baptized him.

PETER'S IMPORTANT LESSON

ACTS 10:1-16, 19-45; 11:1-4,18

A man named Cornelius lived in Caesarea. He was the captain of a unit of Roman soldiers, and he worshiped God, even though he was not a Jew. One day, God sent an angel to visit Cornelius. The angel said, "God has heard your prayers, Cornelius. Send some messengers to Joppa to find a man named Simon Peter. He will tell you how to be saved." Cornelius did what the angel said.

The next day, the messengers arrived in Joppa, where Peter was staying with a friend. Meanwhile, Peter was up on the roof of his friend's house, praying. He was very hungry. As Peter was praying, he had a vision. He saw a huge sheet that was coming down from heaven. The sheet was full of all kinds of animals that were unclean and forbidden for God's people to eat according to the Law of Moses.

A voice came from heaven and said, "Peter, get up! Kill and eat."

"I can't!" Peter answered. "Lord, I have never eaten anything that is unclean in my entire life."

"Do not call anything unclean that God has called clean," the voice answered.

The vision repeated itself two more times, and then the sheet was taken back up into heaven.

Peter was still thinking about his vision when the Holy Spirit told him, "Go downstairs. There are some messengers looking for you. I sent them here, so go with them."

Peter went down and met the messengers at the door. "I am the one you came to find," he said. "What do you want?"

"We have come from Captain Cornelius," the messengers answered. "He is a good man. He worships God and has a good relationship with the Jewish people. Yesterday, God sent an angel to Cornelius and told him to send us to find you so you could come and tell us how to be saved."

The next day, Peter went back with the messengers to Cornelius's house. Cornelius had invited his close friends and family to hear what Peter had to say. Peter told them, "I see now that God loves all people and is happy when anyone worships and obeys Him, no matter where they're from. He has given me the same message for you as for the Jews: Jesus Christ has come to give us peace with God. He forgives people for their sins if only they believe in Him." While Peter was still talking to Cornelius and the people in his house, the Holy Spirit came and filled everyone who was listening.

When the other apostles and believers heard that non-Jewish people had believed God's message, some of them argued with Peter, telling him that he shouldn't have gone into Cornelius's house. But when Peter explained everything that had happened, they stopped their arguments and said, "This must be God's work! He has given life to the Gentiles, too!"

PETER ESCAPES FROM PRISON
ACTS 12:1-17

Before long, King Herod started causing trouble for the believers. He arrested James, the brother of John, and had him beheaded. When Herod saw that the Jewish leaders were happy about this, he arrested Peter, too. He put Peter in prison with four groups of soldiers guarding him and planned to put him on trial. While Peter was in prison, he and the other believers prayed night and day for God's help.

The night before the trial, Peter was sleeping, chained to two guards. There were soldiers guarding the door of the prison, too. Suddenly, an angel appeared, and light filled the whole jail cell. The angel nudged Peter and said, "Get up!" Peter woke up and the chains fell off his hands. "Get dressed," the angel said. "Make sure you have your sandals." After Peter did what the angel told him, the angel said, "Get your coat and come with me."

Peter thought he was dreaming. He followed the angel out of the prison, past all the guards, all the way to the gate of the city. The gate opened on its own, and Peter walked into the street. Once Peter was free, the angel vanished.

When Peter realized that he had really been rescued, he said, "God must have sent that angel to save me from what Herod and the Jewish leaders had planned." He made his way to the house of Mary, Mark's mother, where many other believers had gathered to pray for him. When he knocked on the door, a young servant girl named Rhoda answered it. She heard Peter's voice and ran back into the house, forgetting to open the door for him.

"Peter is outside!" she told the others.

"You're seeing things," they answered.

But Peter kept knocking on the door until they came and let him in. When they saw him, they were speechless. Peter joined them and told them all about how God had rescued him from prison. When he had finished, he left for a nearby city.

ACTS 14:8-20; 16:16-34; 20:17-38; 21:27-36; 22:23-24; 24:24-27; 25:8-12; 27:1-44; 28:11-31

After Saul believed in Jesus, he changed his name to Paul and went around teaching people about Jesus. Once, Paul was in a town in Turkey called Lystra with his friend Barnabas. The people of Lystra worshiped the false gods of Greece. One of the men listening to Paul and Barnabas teach was crippled and couldn't walk. Paul saw that he had faith in Jesus, so he told the man, "Get up!" The man jumped to his feet and the crowd started shouting in their own language, calling Paul and Barnabas Hermes and Zeus because they had performed such a great miracle. They took Paul and Barnabas to their temple of Zeus because they thought the two men were gods, and they wanted to offer a sacrifice.

When Paul and Barnabas found out what was going on, they were very upset. "What are you doing?" they asked. "We're not gods! We are just ordinary people like you! Stop worshiping these false gods and believe in the God who made the land and the sky and the sea and everything else in the whole world."

Even though they kept telling the people the truth, many still wanted to offer a sacrifice to them anyway. Some Jewish leaders from nearby towns were angry about Paul's message. They stoned Paul and dragged him out of the town. The Jewish leaders thought he was dead, but when a group of believers had gathered around Paul, he got back up and returned to the town.

Another time, Paul and his friend Silas were teaching people in Philippi. A young slave girl there had an evil spirit living in her that let her tell people about the future. Her owners made a lot of money from her abilities as a medium. She was following Paul and Silas around, shouting, "These men are servants of the Most High God! They are telling you how to be saved!"

After days of this, Paul was so tired of listening to her yelling that he turned around and told the spirit, "In the name of Jesus Christ, I order you to come out of her!" The evil spirit came out right away and the girl was quiet.

When the girl's owners realized that they couldn't make money from her fortune telling anymore, they dragged Paul and Silas to the town judges. "These men are Jews who have been disturbing everyone in the city," they said. "They are telling us to do things that are illegal for Roman citizens to do."

The rest of the crowd joined in with the accusers, and the judges ordered soldiers to whip Paul and Silas and throw them in prison. The jailer took them into the deepest cell and put their legs in stocks.

That night, Paul and Silas were praying and singing songs of praise to God, and all the other prisoners were listening. About midnight, there was an earthquake and the prison shook. The prison doors popped open and the chains fell off the prisoners. When the jailer woke up and saw that the doors were open, he was afraid that the prisoners had escaped. He drew his sword to kill himself so he wouldn't have to suffer the punishment for losing his prisoners, but Paul shouted, "Don't hurt yourself! We're all still here."

The jailer got a torch and went into the prison. It was just like Paul had said, everyone was still there. He fell down on his knees in front of Paul and Silas and said, "Sirs, what must I do to be saved?"

"Believe in the Lord Jesus and you will be saved," they answered. "Anyone in your home who believes will be saved, too!" The jailer led them out of the prison and took them to his home. He cleaned their injuries while they told him and his family about Jesus. Then he and everyone in his house believed in Jesus, and Paul and Silas baptized them.

Paul had been traveling for a long time, and he felt God's Spirit telling him it was time to go back to Jerusalem. Many of the people he had met in his travels gathered at the harbor city of Miletus to say goodbye.

He told them, "I have always tried to serve the Lord with humility, even though many Jewish leaders have been causing trouble for me. Whenever I taught, I always tried to teach everyone how to be saved, whether they were Jews or Gentiles. I always taught you that you must turn away from your sins and believe in Jesus.

"I don't know what is going to happen to me in Jerusalem, but God is telling me to go there. God has warned me over and over that I will be arrested and have a lot of trouble, but God's message is more important than even my life. As long as I do the work that Jesus has given me to do, I will be content. My work is to tell people about God's kindness and salvation."

When he had finished speaking to them, Paul and his friends prayed together. He hugged them all and said, "You won't see me again."

When Paul finally reached the temple in Jerusalem, a crowd of Jewish leaders from the areas he had been traveling in arrived. They stirred up the crowd to attack him. "This man has been going around telling everyone bad things about Israel and the Law and the temple," they said. "He even brought his unclean Gentile friends into the temple!" They said this because they had seen Paul in Jerusalem with some Gentile believers, and they thought he had brought them into the temple, which was against the Law.

The crowd was so upset that they grabbed Paul, dragged him out of the temple, and started beating him. They wanted to kill him, but a Roman general heard about the riot and brought some soldiers to stop it.

The general arrested Paul and tried to figure out what he had done to make the crowd so angry. The crowd was

shouting so many different things that he couldn't figure out what they were saying, so he ordered his soldiers to take Paul to the Roman fortress. The crowd followed them, shouting, "Kill him! Kill him!" The soldiers had to carry Paul into the fortress to keep the crowd away from him.

Paul stayed in a prison that was near Jerusalem until the governor could hear his case. Governor Felix and his wife Drusilla went to the prison to speak with him, and Paul told them all about Jesus and how to be saved through faith in Him. Felix was afraid when he heard some of what Paul had to say about doing what's right and the judgment at the end of time, so he said, "I don't have time to talk now, but I want to hear more about this. I will send for you again." From then on, Felix talked to Paul frequently, but not because he wanted to learn. Felix was hoping Paul would offer him a bribe.

Two years passed, then a man named Festus became governor instead of Felix. Festus invited Paul to explain himself. Paul said, "I did not break any of the laws of my own people or of Rome, and I have not done anything against the temple or the emperor."

Festus believed Paul, but he also wanted to make the Jewish leaders happy. He said, "Will you go to Jerusalem so I can hold a trial about these things?"

Paul knew that the Jewish leaders had made plans to kill him as soon as he arrived in Jerusalem, so he said, "I am in the emperor's courtroom right now, and that is where my trial should be. You and I both know that I didn't do anything against my fellow Jews. If I had committed a crime, I wouldn't try to escape the consequences. But I am innocent, and no one can legally hand me over to these people who want to kill me. I want my case to be tried by the emperor himself."

Festus talked to his advisors about what to do. Since Paul was a Roman citizen, Festus told him, "If you want to be tried by the emperor, you will go to the emperor!"

Paul and some of his companions set sail for Rome. He was guarded by Roman soldiers. On the way to Rome, they reached a place called Fair Havens. Winter had come, and the water was dangerous, so Paul warned the crew not to sail until the weather was safe again. He said, "If we sail now, the ship and cargo will be lost, along with many lives." But the captain and the owner of the ship didn't want to spend the winter in Fair Havens, so they tried to sail further down the coast.

At first, it seemed like they had made the right choice. The wind was gentle and the water was calm. Then a strong wind picked up and made it impossible to control the ship. For two long weeks they were tossed around by the strong wind and storms. Finally, the sailors saw that they

were close to land. They didn't want to be smashed on rocks, so they let down the anchors and waited for morning.

In the morning, the sailors saw a beach they didn't recognize, and they decided to try to make it to shore. They cut off the anchors, raised the sail, and sailed the ship towards the beach. The ship ran aground on a sandbank, and the waves started to smash it. The captain ordered everyone to jump into the water and swim for shore or float on pieces of wood. Because of this, they all made it safely to shore.

In the spring, Paul and his companions found a new ship that was headed to Rome from the island where they had been shipwrecked. This time, the ship arrived safely. While he was living in Rome and waiting for his trial, Paul had to live in a house with a soldier guarding him to make sure he didn't escape. He was allowed to have visitors in the house, so he gathered some of the Jewish leaders of Rome.

"My friends," Paul told them, "I have never done anything to hurt the Jews, and I have never broken any of our laws or customs. Even so, some of the Jewish leaders in Jerusalem handed me over to the Romans, claiming that I deserved to die. The Roman governor wanted to release me, but the Jewish leaders tried to have me brought back to Jerusalem. I asked to be judged by the emperor, and that is why I am here. I have called you all here to tell you about something amazing."

The Jewish leaders said. "We believe you mean no harm, and we want to hear what you have to say. If this is about the believers in Jesus, we have heard that many people are against that group, and we want to know more."

Paul met with the Jewish leaders in Rome and taught them about Jesus. He used the Law of Moses and the writings of the Prophets to convince them to believe that Jesus is the Messiah they had been waiting for for so long. Some of them believed him, but others did not. Because they didn't all agree, they stopped coming to meet with Paul. Paul said, "You may have rejected this message, but God wants to save the Gentiles, too. They will listen!" Paul lived in Rome for two years, teaching people about Jesus in his house. He was brave enough to keep preaching about God's kingdom no matter what, and no one tried to stop him.

A PROMISE FOR THE FUTURE

REVELATION 1:9-18; 21:1-4; 22:20

The apostle John also continued to teach people about Jesus, and because of that, he was imprisoned and exiled to an island called Patmos. While he was there, John had a vision. He heard a voice that was as loud as a trumpet. When he turned around, he saw someone who looked like the Son of Man standing in the middle of seven golden lamp stands.

It was Jesus! He was wearing a long robe with a golden sash, and His hair was as white as snow. His eyes blazed like fire, and His feet were

glowing like hot metal. His voice sounded like a waterfall, and He held seven stars in His right hand. There was a sharp sword coming out of His mouth, and His face was shining brighter than the sun. When John saw Him, he fell down at His feet. Jesus reached down and touched him, and said, "Don't be afraid! I am the beginning and the end. I am the one who died, but now I am alive forever."

Jesus showed John a vision of the end of the world, when He will come back to judge the world and rescue His people once and for all. After everything else in John's vision, Jesus showed him a new heaven

and a new earth to replace the old heaven and earth, which would be destroyed. In the middle of the new heaven and earth, there was a holy city, the New Jerusalem. It was as beautiful as a bride on her wedding day.

Jesus told John, "God's home will be with His people. He will live with them and they will be His own again, just like He wanted from the beginning. They will live with Him, loving Him and being loved by Him in a perfect relationship forever. He will wipe away their tears, and there will be no more death or suffering or crying or pain anymore. All those things will be gone for good. I promise that I am coming soon!"

"Yes, Lord Jesus," John said. "Please come back soon!"

God's promises when you are:

Afraid
Psa 4:8; 23:4; Isa 35:4; Rom 8:37-39; 2 Cor 1:10; 2 Tim 1:7; Heb 13:6

Anxious
Psa 55:22; Isa 41:13; Matt 6:25; 11:28-30; Phil 4:6-7; 1 Pet 5:7

Confused
Psa 32:8; Isa 42:16; John 8:12; John 14:27;

Dejected
Matt 11:28-30; Heb 4:16;

Depressed
Deu 31:8; Psa 34:18-19; Isa 49:13-15

Despairing
Psa 119:116; Heb 10:35-36

Disappointed
Psa 22:4-5;

Discouraged
Jos 1:9;

Grieving
Psa 119:76-77; Jer 31:13; Matt 5:4; 1 Th 4:13-14; Rev 21:3-4

Impatient
Psa 27:13-14; 37:4-5; Rom 2:7; Heb 10:35-36

Needy
Isa 58:11; 2 Cor 9:10-12; Eph 3:20-21; Phil 4:19; Psa 37:4-5; 103:5; Luke 12:29-31

Obedient
John 14:21-23; Jas 1:25

Persecuted
Gen 50:20; Psa 37:1-2; Matt 5:10-12; 2 Cor 4:8-11;

Sick
Psa 23:4; 73:26; Matt 8:16-17; Rom 8:37-39; Jas 5:14-15

Suffering
Psa 34:19; John 16:33; Rom 8:16-18; 1 Pet 2:20-21; 4:12-13

Tempted
1 Cor 10:13; Heb 2:18; 4:15-16; Jas 1:2-3,13-14; 1 Pet 5:8-10

Weak
Psa 72:12-14; Isa 41:10; Rom 8:26; 2 Cor 4:7-9; 12:9-10

What the Bible says about:

Addiction
Pro 23:29-35; Rom 6:1-14; 12:1-2; 1 Cor 6:12-20; Phil 3:17-19

Ambitions
Mark 9:33-35; 10:35-45; Phil 2:1-5; 3:12-14

Anger
Gen 4:1-12; Psa 4:4; Pro 16:32; Matt 5:22; Eph 4:25-27; Jas 1:19-20

Anxiety
Psa 94:17-19; Ecc 2:22-25; Luke 12:22-24; Phil 4:4-9; Heb 13:5-6

Apathy
Ecc 9:10; Matt 25:1-13; Luke 12:35-48; 1 Th 5:1-11; Rev 3:1-6; 3:14-22

Assurance of salvation
Psa 91:14-16; Mic 7:18-19; John 3:14-21; 11:25-26; Acts 16:31-34; 1 John 5:9-13

Baptism
Matt 28:16-20; Luke 7:29-30; Acts 8:12; 8:35-39; 10:44-48; 19:4-7; 22:16; Rom 6:1-8

Bible reading
Jos 1:7-8; Neh 8:1-6; Psa 1:1-2; 2 Tim 3:14-17; Heb 4:12; Jas 1:22-25

Bitterness
Psa 73; Pro 16:32; 1 Cor 13:4-7; Eph 4:29-32; 5:1-2; Heb 12:14-15

Blood of Jesus
Matt 26:27-29; Heb 9:11-28

Body of Christ
1 Cor 12:12-31; Heb 2:14-18

Celibacy
Matt 19:11-12; 1 Cor 7:32-35;

Cheating
Gen 27:41; Matt 18:15-17; 1 Cor 6:1-8; Jas 5:1-9

Children
Psa 78:5-7; 127:3-4; 128:1-4; Matt 18:1-7; Mark 10:13-16; Eph 6:1-4

Comfort
tIsa 12:1-2; 40:1-11; 2 Cor 1:3-7; 7:6-7

Compassion
Ps 103:8-12; Psa 116:5-6; Mic 6:8; John 11:17-44; 2 Cor 1:3-7; 1 John 3:11-24

Contentment
Pro 15:15-17; Matt 6:33; 2 co 12:8-10; 1 Tim 6:6-10; Heb 13:5-6

Conversion
Deu 4:30-31; 2 Ch 7:14; Ez 18:30-32; John 3:1-21; 2 Cor 5:17-19; Eph 2:1-10

Creation
Gen 1-2; Psa 8; Psa 19; Psa 104; Rom 1:18-23; Rom 8:18-27; Col 1:15-17

Death
Psa 116:15; Isa 57:1-2; John 12:23-26; Rom 6:1-14; 1 Cor 15

Disagreements
Matt 7:1-5; Rom 12:9-21; 14:1; 15:7; 2 Cor 5:11-12

Discipleship
Luke 14:25-33;

Discipline
Pro 3:11-12; 13:24; Heb 12:1-13; Rev 3:19

Divorce
Deu 24:1-4; Mal 2:13-16; Matt 19:1-12; Mark 10:2-12; 1 Cor 7:10-16

Eternal life
Job 19:25-27; Matt 19:16-30; John 3:1-21; Rom 6: 23

Faith
Gen 15:1-6; Psa 119:65-72; Pro 3:5-10; Rom 3:21; 5:1 Heb 11:1

Faithfulness
Gen 39:2-4; 1 Sa 17:36-37; 1 Ki 3:5-9;

Fellowship
Psa 95:1-7; Acts 2:42-47; Heb 10:19-25

Forgiveness
Lev 16:2-34; Isa 6:1-7; Rom 3:21-26; 2 Cor 5:14-21; Heb 9; 1 Pet 2:22-25; Matt 6:14-15; 18:21-22; Col 3:12-14; Jas 2:12-13

Freedom
John 8:31-42; Rom 8:1-17; Gal 4:21 – 5:26

Friendship
Pro 17:17; Pro 27:6; Ecc 4:9-12; John15:17;

Generosity
Deu 15:7-11; Pro 3:9; Matt 6:1-4

God's guidance
1 Ki 3:5-10; Pro 2:1-6; Rom 12:1-2; Eph 5:15-17; Jas 1:5-8

Grace
Psa 86; Psa 103; Mic 7:18-20; Luke 15:11-31; Rom 5; Eph 2

Greed
1 Ki 21:1-22; Pro 15:27; Luke 12:13-21; 1 Tim 6:3-10; Jas 5:1-6; Ecc 2:1-11; 2 Cor 9:6-15; Eph 5:3-7; 1 John 3:16-18

Guilt
Psa 130:1-6; Rom 8:1-2; 1 Cor 6:11; Heb 10:22-23

Happiness
Psa 33; Isa 12; Isa 52:7-10; Matt 5:1-12; Luke 15; Phil 4:4-9; Jas 1:2-18; 1 Pet 4:12-19

Heaven
1 Ki 8:23-30; Isa 65:17-25; Matt 6:19-24; Matt 25:31-46; Phil 3:12 – 4:1; Rev 21

Hope for the future
Lam 3:22-26;; 1 Pet 1:3-9; 5:10-11; Rev 11:15-18

Hospitality
Gen 18:1-8; 2 Sam 9:1-7; Luke 14:12-14; Rom 12:13; 1 Pet 4:9

Hypocrisy
Isa 1:10-15; Zak 7:2-14; Matt 6:1-24; Matt 23; Jas 1:22-27

Jealousy
Pro23:17-18; Gal 5:13-15; Jas 3:13-18

Joy
Rom 5:1-11; 1 Pet 1:3-9

Judging others
Matt 7:1-5; 1 Cor 4:1-5; Jas 2:1-13; Jas 4:11-12

Justification
Gen 15:1-6; Isa 53; Rom 3:21-31; Rom 4:1 – 5:11; Gal 2:15-21

Laziness
Pro 6:6-11; 1 Th 4:11-12; 2 Th 3:9-13

Loneliness
1 Ki 19:1-18; Matt 26:36-46; 2 Tim 4:16-18

Love
Lev 19:18+34; Deu 6:1-5; Sng 1-2; Mark 12:28-34; 1 Cor 13; 1 John 4:7-21

Lust
Matt 5:27-32; 1 Cor 6:18-20; 7:2-5; Rom 13:8-10; Jas 1:13-15

Marriage
Gen 2:19-25; Ecc 9:7-10; Matt 19:4-12; 1 Cor 7; Eph 5:22-27; 1 Tim 4:1-5

Peace
Num 6:24-26; Isa 9:2-7; John 14:25-27; Rom 5:1-11; Eph 2:14-18; Phil 4:4-9

Poverty
Deu 15:4-11; Amos 5:10-15; Matt 25:31-46; Luke 1:46-55; Jas 2:1-13

Powers of darkness
Jos 1:6-9; Psa 56:1-4; Rom 8:38-39; Eph 6:10-18; 2 Tim 4:3-5

Prayer
2 Ch 6:13-42; 20:5-12; Matt 6:5-15; Mark 11:22-26; Luke 18:9-14; Phil 4:4-7

Pride
2 Sam 22:28; Psa 31:23; Dan 5:18-20; Rom 12:3; Phil 2:3-11

Profanity
Ex 20:7; Pro 30:10-14; Matt 5:33-37; Eph 4:29-32; Heb 6:16-17; Jas 3:1-12

Quarreling
Gen 13:5-11; 2 Tim 2:14; Jas 4:1-3

Reconciliation
Gen 33:1-4; Gen 50:15-21; Matt 5:23-26; 2 Cor 5:16-21; Eph 2:11-22

Repentance2
Ch 7:14; Ez 18:30-32; Matt 4:17; Luke 18:9-14; Acts 2:38-41

Responsibility
Luke 7:1-10; Gal 6:9-10

Resurrection
Job 19:23-27; Psa 16; Dan 12:1-4; Matt 27:57 – 28:20; 1 Cor 15

Return of Christ
Matt 24; John 14:1-4; 1 Cor 15:12-28; 1 Th 4:13 – 5:11

Revenge
Deu 32:34-35; Psa 94:1; Pro 25:21-22; Matt 5:38-42; Rom 12:17-19; 1 Pet 3:8-14

Reward
Isa 61:8-9; Matt 5:3-12; Mark 10:29-31; 1 Cor 3:10-15

Salvation
Ex 15:1-18; Psa 62; Luke 19:1-10; Acts 16:16-34; Eph 2:1-10

Sanctification
2 Cor 7:1; 1 Th 5:23; 2 Pet 1:3-11

Self-control
Ps 39:1; Pro 10:19-21; Jas 3:1-12

Spiritual gifts
Rom 12:6-8; 1 Cor 1:4-9; 12:1 – 14:25; 1 Pet 4:7-11

Suffering
Deu 8:1-5; Job 1-2; Psa 77; Isa 53; Rom 8:12-28; 1 Pet 3:8-22; 1 Pet 4:12-19

Temptations
Gen 3:1-7; Ecc 2:1-11; 2 Cor 6:14; 7:1; Jas 4:4-10; 1 John 2:15-17

The Cross
Mark 8:31 – 9:1; Luke 23:26-49

The Holy Spirit
Isa 61:1-3; Joel 2:28-32; John 14:15-31; John 16:5-16; Acts 2; Rom 8:1-17

The Lord's Supper
Luke 22:7-23; John 13; 1 Cor 11:17-34

Unfaithfulness (Marital)
Ex 20:14; Lev 20:10; Deu 22:22-24; Matt 5:27-32; Gal 5:13-26; Eph 4:17 – 5:3

Unity
Psa 133; John 17; Eph 4:1-16

─── HOW TO GET SAVED ───

God created the world and He created you. The Bible also tells us that He is interested in you and He loves you. (John 3:16)

The problem is that we are sinners, and sin hinders us in having fellowship with God. So God in His love sent Jesus as *"the Lamb of God, who takes away the sins of the world"* (John 1:29).
Jesus never committed any sin. (1 Peter 2:22)
Therefore as the holy Son of God Jesus died for the sins of the whole world.
Three days later God's power made Jesus alive again. Jesus lives today. He loves you and wants to receive any one, who believes and turns to God.

The Bible says in Romans 10:9: *"If you confess with your mouth, "Jesus is Lord," and believe in your heart that God raised him from the dead, you will be saved."* This is God's promise to you even today! If you believe and want to be saved, you can pray this prayer:

Dear Lord Jesus.
I know that I am a sinner, and I ask for your forgiveness.
I believe you died for my sins and rose from the dead.
Thank you that you love me enough to take away my sins.
I turn from my sins and invite you to come into my heart and life.
I want to trust and follow you as my Lord and Savior.
Thank you Jesus. Amen.

(Read more in the Bible – see references in parentheses)

GROW IN FAITH

How do I grow in my faith as a new Christian?

Making a decision to follow Jesus and be His disciple is the best decision you can ever make. He loves you no matter what, and He wishes the best for your life.

To grow in your faith is to learn more about Jesus and His love and to learn to obey Him.

Here are some great things you can do:

1. Read the Bible daily.

The Bible is God's way of speaking to us. (Romans 10:17) It is in a sense His "love letter" to you.

2. Pray daily.

(Matthew 6:9-13)

3. Meet with people who share your faith, such as a church fellowship.

(Hebrew 10:25)

4. Learn to obey God

"Whoever has my commands and obeys them, he is the one who loves me. He who loves me will be loved by my Father, and I too will love him and show myself to him."

John 14:21

NOTES

NOTES

NOTES

NOTES

NOTES

NOTES